"Peter Martyr Vermigli is undoubtedly one of the most significant Reformed theologians of the sixteenth century and his *Common Places* is the crown jewel of his collected works. The rendering of this work into contemporary English is a great service to the understanding of Reformation thought and will be enriching for scholars and pastors alike. Vermigli's theological training and acumen are on full display here and the results are rightly esteemed as a masterwork of Reformed theology."

—JORDAN J. BALLOR

The Acton Institute, Junius Institute, author of Covenant, Causality, and Law: A Study in the Theology of Wolfgang Musculus

"With this precise but grandly readable translation, Reformation scholars owe a debt of gratitude to the editors and translator for this initial volume in this new series on Peter Martyr Vermigli's *Common Places*. Kirk Summers has faithfully and eloquently rendered Vermigli who is here at his subtle and forceful best; and has thus opened to a wider audience the Reformer's thought on some of the questions most central to the disputes of the sixteenth century: sin, human nature, what imputation entails, and even the nature of sacramental grace. Further, Summers's painstaking apparatus (Vermigli often quoted his sources from memory) lays bare Vermigli's vast command of the literature on these questions. Honor due."

—GARY JENKINS

Eastern University; author of Calvin's Tormentor's: Understanding the Conflicts that Shaped the Reformer

"Legend has it that Peter Martyr Vermigli descended out of the Italian Alps as the 'ready-made Reformer,' and his *Common Places* certainly confirm both his reputation and why so many esteemed his work. His *Common Places* were posthumously extracted from his biblical commentaries, which means that they are insightfully exegetical and theological. Students of the Reformation would do well to pick up this book and see for themselves the deep currents that run through his work. Students of Scripture will also greatly profit from one who knows the Bible so well."

—J. V. FESKO

Harriet Barbour Professor of Systematic and Historical Theology, Reformed Theological Seminary, Jackson, Mississippi

"In 1563, not long after the death of Peter Martyr Vermigli in Zurich, Theodore Beza urged on Heinrich Bullinger the need for a systematic theology to be compiled from Vermigli's immense corpus of scriptural commentary—*"eine Dogmatik in nuce."* Owing in good part to Anthony Marten's Elizabethan translation, Vermigli's *Common Places* became one of the most influential of all Reformed systematic theologies, especially in the English-speaking world. Kirk Summers has made a selection of these commonplaces pertaining to the pivotal Christian teaching concerning Original Sin and rendered them into lucid, legible, modern English. For any scholar or aspiring theologian attuned to the Reformed tradition this volume should be obligatory reading."

—W.J. TORRANCE KIRBY

McGill University, author of The Zurich Connection and Tudor Political Theology

"According to Peter Martyr Vermigli, the supreme end and highest good in life is to be justified in Christ, accepted in love by the eternal Father. However, it is impossible to appreciate the significance of this acceptance until one has first grasped the catastrophic problem of original sin, the desolate pit from which God raises sinners to make them saints. In addition to answering critical questions surrounding the doctrine (i.e., What is sin? Who is responsible for it? And how does it spread?), this volume showcases Peter Martyr's convictions on a host of related topics including divine creation, humanity's *infidelitas,* total depravity, sexual relations, *imago Dei,* natural gifts, and the necessity of imputed righteousness as the basis for divine favor."

—CHRIS CASTALDO

Lead Pastor of New Covenant Church, Naperville., author of Justified in Christ: The Doctrines of Peter Martyr Vermigli and John Henry Newman

"Vermigli was one of the most important theologians of the sixteenth century. His *Loci Communes* is a collated summary of his theology and I am delighted to see this part of it made accessible in a new translation to an English speaking readership."

—DR. ROBERT LETHAM

Professor of Systematic & Historical Theology, Union School of Theology, Wales, UK

PETER MARTYR VERMIGLI
COMMON PLACES:

On Free Will & The Law

PETER MARTYR VERMIGLI

COMMON PLACES:

ON FREE WILL
& THE LAW

Translated and edited by Joseph A. Tipton

DAVENANT PRESS 2024

ISBN: 1-949716-36-8
ISBN-13: 978-1-949716-36-8

Cover design and typesetting by
Rachel Rosales, Orange Peal Design

TABLE OF CONTENTS

VOLUME INTRODUCTION

Joseph A. Tipton

The present volume comprises chapters two and three of the second book of Peter Martyr Vermigli's *Common Places*.[1] These chapters offer a broad selection of the Italian Reformer's thinking on matters pertaining to the topics of free will and the law. Yet it would be unfair to the Reformer to attempt to evaluate his thinking on these subjects on the basis of what is contained in these two chapters alone. Being extracts compiled by Robert Masson[2] for the first edition of the *Common Places* (printed in London in 1576) and taken from various biblical commentaries Vermigli composed throughout his lifetime, they are oriented to specific biblical passages and to questions those passages

---

1. Vermigli's discussion of free will and the law follows his treatment of original sin in the first chapter. One can see why Vermigli's editors decided upon this sequence, since the idea of the bondage of man's will is the logical result of his fall and subsequent enslavement to sin.

2. Robert Masson, or Robert le Maçon, Sieur de la Fontaine, was the Huguenot minister of the French congregation in London at the time. His involvement in the compilation of Vermigli's *Loci* speaks to the latter's influence on both English and French Protestants. For the printing history of the *Loci* see Joseph C. McClelland, "A Literary History of the *Loci Communes*," in *A Companion to Peter Martyr Vermigli*, ed. Torrance Kirby, Emilio Campi, and Frank A. James III (Leiden: Brill, 2009), 489.

raised for Vermigli, and at many a point they betray this exegetical orientation. Exegesis is notoriously different than
a formal treatment. That said, there still clearly emerges
from these chapters a coherent set of ideas distinctive to
Vermigli and his generation of Reformers that deserve special attention, especially with regard to free will.

First, Vermigli's method deserves attention. For cen-
turies before Vermigli, Western Christianity approached
such topics as free will and the law through the analytical
apparatus developed by the Scholastic theologians of the
High Middle Ages. This approach involved the application of rigorous logic within a tight framework of question and response in an effort to reconcile apparent con-
tradictions, especially those between the Bible and what
survived of Aristotle's writings, which were transmitted
to Europe via Arabic translations. It was a philosophi-
co-theological approach, making use of a special brand of
Latin developed to convey the precise jargon Scholastic
disputations required.

Vermigli, on the other hand, lived and worked on
the other side of Italian humanism. This movement, with
notable exceptions,[3] discarded the Scholastic approach in
favor of one based on the rhetorical canons of Cicero and
Quintilian. The result was not just a more classical Latin,
but the use of a wider swathe of source material going
far beyond the Aristotelian corpus; a close, philological
reading of biblical passages with a view to the context
and rhetorical aim of the writer (a technique referred to

---

3. E.g., Giovanni Pico della Mirandola and Piero Pomponazzi moved
in humanist circles yet continued to employ Scholastic method to
good effect.

as "logical analysis" by Irena Backus);[4] and a preference for commentary over theological treatise, all conveyed in a conversational, yet decidedly rhetorical, tone.[5] Hence Vermigli shares with his humanist compatriots a discursive style that moves easily from topic to topic, question to question.

On the subject of source material, many have observed that the humanists did not fault the Scholastics for their slavish obsession with *an* ancient authority, but rather for their slavish obsession with *one* ancient authority. The humanists had this in common with the Scholastics: the development of their ideas typically involved analyzing what ancient authorities said rather than blazing new trails. The humanists preferred to range over a wider spectrum of ancient authors instead of fixating on just one or two. This humanist method could manifest itself in various forms. In the hands of thinkers like Lorenzo Valla, it proved to be an incisive tool for examining complex questions, assessing past ideas, and arriving at startlingly novel answers that often problematized an entire tradition. Often, however, it amounted to little more than essays with

---

4. Irena Backus, "Biblical Hermeneutics and Exegesis," in *The Oxford Encyclopedia of the Reformation*, ed. Hans J. Hillebrand, 1:152–58. Also, Irena Backus, "Piscator Misconstrued? Some Remarks on Robert Rollock's Logical Analysis of Hebrews IX," in "Text, Translation and Exegesis of Hebrews IX: Papers Presented at a Seminar Held at the IHR, Geneva on 14–15 June 1982," special issue, *Journal of Medieval and Renaissance Studies* (Spring 1984): 113–19.

5. See, for example, Vermigli's use of *hypophora* and *peritropē* in *On Free Will*, section 9, and *prosopopoeia* in *On Free Will*, section 21 (and the footnotes accompanying those sections).

a wide range of citations lifted from antiquity to serve as proof-texts for one's position.

Vermigli discusses free will and the law in this humanist strain. He examines a long list of patristic writers and what they said on any given subject, and, in the end, he expresses his agreement with one. This approach is effective to varying degrees. It sometimes involves grappling with a single text and evaluating its importance, or even authenticity, along philological lines, as when Vermigli discusses a homily supposed to be by Chrysostom but whose authenticity he doubts because it is both self-contradictory and inconsistent with other works agreed to be by Chrysostom (*On Free Will,* section 14). Alternatively, it at times involves nothing more than citing authorities secondhand through Peter Lombard or the *Decretum Gratiani* (cf. chapter 3, section 9) and weighing what one Father said over against another.

Thus, when it comes to locating the *form* Vermigli's discourse takes, he is to be placed within this broad humanist exegetical tradition. On the other hand, when it comes to locating the tradition within which his *thought* should be placed, the situation becomes a little more complicated. While thinking in the West on free will is a subject of enormous dimensions, a useful paradigm was offered by the German historian of philosophy Heinz Heimsoeth in the first quarter of the twentieth century.[6]

---

6. *Die Sechs Grossen Themen des Abendländishen Metaphysik und der Ausgang des Mittelalters* (Berlin: G. Stilke, 1922), 279–343, translated into English as Heinz Heimsoeth, *The Six Great Themes of Western Metaphysics and the End of the Middle Ages,* trans. Ramon Betanzos (Detroit: Wayne State University Press, 1994), 224–68. Any citations to this work will be in the more recent English translation.

Heimsoeth categorized the major Western philosophical traditions according to their response to the problem of the individual's decision-making. They either privileged the intellect or regarded the will as the primary organ of human deliberation, and so of action, too. Heimsoeth quite naturally places the Greeks squarely in the intellectual tradition. In general, they regarded all human decision-making as ratiocinative. Given the requisite data, the mind chooses a course of action based on that information, and the will follows obediently; in fact, it "automatically abides by the outcome."[7] So subservient and passive was the role the will was relegated to that in many of their discussions it often amounts to little more than desire, or a certain species of desire, rather than a discrete function of human psychology.[8] This general attitude manifests itself specifically in Socrates's dictum that "nobody errs willingly" (on the grounds that everybody aims at the good; if anybody chooses a course of action that leads to what is detrimental, the cause must have been ignorance, because no one would willfully invite harm to oneself), as well as Aristotle's explanation of *akrasia* (the phenomenon of deciding to do something against one's better judgment) as failure to rightly apply the minor premise in a practical syllogism. For instance, if the major premise is, "Things sweet are to be avoided," and the minor premise is, "This particular thing is sweet," the conclusion is, "This particular thing is to be avoided." If one admits the veracity of the major premise, yet gobbles down a candy bar anyway,

---

7. Heimsoeth, *Western Metaphysics*, 225.

8. Heimsoeth, *Western Metaphysics*, 243.

they, according to Aristotle, have experienced an intellective problem concerning the minor premise.[9] In this way the Greek tradition on this topic was heavily weighted towards the primacy of the intellect over a very downgraded conceptualization of the will.

Heimsoeth then explores the early Christian, and specifically New Testament, view of decision-making and finds it to be a complete reversal of the Greek tradition. There the phenomenon of acting against one's better judgment, of knowing what the good thing to do is, yet *willfully* refusing to do it (cf. Romans 7), indicates that early Christian thinking not only elevated the will and the role it plays in the human psychology to the status of a discrete function, but even gave it primacy over the intellect. Knowing what the good is offers little benefit; what matters is that one *want* it, and only God's active intervention to reorient the individual's will can cause him to want it. On a related note, Heimsoeth finds that the New Testament privileging of love over knowledge, *agape* over *gnosis*, is of a piece with this new emphasis on the will, since now the end-goal of life is not idle contemplation, but active communion with others and with God.[10]

After discussing how thinkers in the post-apostolic age reverted to the Greek tradition and their prioritizing the intellective side of deliberation, where pride of place goes to Origen, he dwells at length on Augustine, whose thinking on the will brought fundamental changes not

---

9. Cf. Risto Saarinen, *The Weakness of the Will in Medieval Thought: From Augustine to Buridan* (Leiden: Brill, 1994), 9–10.

10. Heimsoeth, *Western Metaphysics*, 227–28.

just to theology, but to all subsequent Western thought. In short, Augustine restored New Testament anthropology to Christianity. Determining that *omnes nihil aliud quam voluntates sunt* (all people are nothing but wills), he completely inverted the relationship of willing and knowing. Whereas the Greek tradition regarded action as resulting from the mind's reaching a verdict on a given set of data, then relaying to the will what the appropriate steps to take are, Augustine regarded the will as the primary driver of virtually all of human action—even to the point of determining what the mind knows. "A person does not love what he has come to know correctly, but rather," Heimsoeth interprets Augustine, "he tries to know whatever he inwardly inclines toward."[11] This means that the will is extremely influential on, if not determinative of, what the mind knows, as it plays a decisive role in selecting and directing what the mind will apprehend.[12] Therefore, the will is not only a discrete, but indeed an independent function that is not worked upon by the intellect or any other organ; it is a spontaneous power working upon the intellect.

Thus, in one sense, the will for Augustine is absolutely free, the prime mover of all the individual's affections, intellections, and actions. Yet it is this very absolute freedom that, paradoxically, explains the will's bondage.

---

11. Heimsoeth, *Western Metaphysics*, 232.

12. Heimsoeth, *Western Metaphysics*, 232: This being the case, Heimsoeth remarks, knowledge requires less understanding and more attention (Aufmerksamkeit) to focus the mind on the data from which learning is to take place. Needless to say, Heimsoeth does not see Buridan's ass posing any real paradox for Augustine.

Due to original sin, the will has been re-oriented away from God, a movement that means the individual is completely alienated from God, since returning to God would require the will to cease to be the will. Needless to say, the individual's noetic powers cannot help, since they are powerless against the will; indeed, they are subordinate to it (thus authenticating the phenomenon of *akrasia* and the experience described by Paul in Romans 7 much more than previous thinking on the subject). So complete is this alienation from God that it is irreversible *as far as the individual's own powers are concerned*. Therefore, the only possibility of reorienting the individual back to God is God's grace—hence that heavy emphasis on grace in Augustine that earned him the moniker *doctor gratiae*. Yet it is to be noted that this robust doctrine of grace and election is intimately linked to Augustine's construal of the relationship between intellect and will, will having the clear upper hand.

For Heimsoeth, Western thought eventually reverted to an intellective construal of decision-making in the Scholastic system of Thomas Aquinas. Whereas thinkers such as Henry of Ghent, the Victorines, Duns Scotus, and William of Ockham represent important developments in voluntaristic interpretation of both human and divine deliberation, it was Aristotelian Thomism that carried the day.[13]

Now, to return to Vermigli and his treatment of the will, his approach is perhaps best characterized as eclectic, a blend of the Aristotelian intellectualist construal with

13. Heimsoeth, *Western Metaphysics*, 238–44.

the Augustinian voluntarism. He begins his discussion of the will in good form with a definition:

> Accordingly, the will is free when it embraces, as it likes, those decisions which are approved by the cognitive part of the mind. Thus, the nature of free will, while most evident in volition, has its roots in reason and those who wish to use this faculty correctly must above all see to it that there occur no error in their reasoning. Error usually occurs in two ways: We either fail to see what is just and unjust in the performance of our actions; or, if we see it, we err in our examination of the reasons that are brought forward for either side, for desire in us nearly always favors the weaker argument. This is why the stronger and better position is often dismissed and rejected. We see this sometimes happening in debates: Those who wish to defend the weaker side tend to adorn it with every sort of rhetorical flourish and embellishment so that the audience will be attracted to the polish and allure and not weigh the strength and soundness of the reasoning (*On Free Will*, section 1).

Here at the outset it is clear that Vermigli regards the intellect as primary over the will. The correct use of the will involves correct thinking beforehand. The will is the passive receptor of directives sent to it from the *nous*. This relationship is borne out in the way he describes error. Error, he says, is either failure in intellectual perception or the derailing of the mind by desire. This "desire" (*cupiditas*) appears in this passage to be distinct from the will (*voluntas*), not a function of it, a *tertium quid* that intercepts information coming from the mind, distorts it, and uses specious argumentation and rhetorical flourish to cause the will to espouse the logically less cogent. Yet it is not that the will is choosing to go against the mind; it is simply deceived. It thinks what it chooses is coming from the mind. It is all still a cognitive process.[14]

Just as error is the result of a faulty noetic process, so conversion is conceived of as the successful result of an intellective moment. Augustinian in his denial that salvation can be achieved by anyone or anything other than God, Vermigli characterizes conversion as a point at which the darkened mind is illuminated:

> For just as some truths are so obvious that the mind cannot but give its assent to them, in the same way, when God's presence is revealed and made apparent, so great is his goodness that the saints are unable to withdraw from it. In this way, although we necessarily sin before being reborn in Christ, the rights of our will are still not violated, since whatever we do, we do both willingly and driven by some motivation (section 6).

For Vermigli, conversion occurs not when the will is finally delivered from its rebellion and is turned toward God in love and genuine willingness, but rather when a reve-

---

14. Cf. section 24, where Vermigli repeats his point in different words: "The strength of the affections and all the mind's focus are concentrated on the reasons that argue for pleasures and desire."

lation of God's presence is, one feels, almost forced upon the benighted mind, at which point the sinner perceives God's goodness as never before. Simultaneously, the will remains as passive a receptor as Aristotle ever conceived of it, for once the new information of God's goodness is merely presented to the sinner's mind he cannot but gravitate to it; or, to use Vermigli's language, he is "unable to withdraw from it."

Thus, as Vermigli makes clear at the outset of his discussion, the overall framework within which he examines the will owes a great deal to the Greek intellectual tradition. Structurally, *nous* controls the will, so much so that in order for the will to be directed properly this way or that, the darkness of the mind needs to be dispelled, and the will then follows automatically. This position is not a far cry from one of the key ideas in Socrates's thinking that "Nobody errs willingly."

Yet, as his treatment of the will progresses, Vermigli moves seamlessly into an Augustinian formulation of decision-making. This becomes clear as early as section two, where Vermigli lays out the parameters within which the will is active. There are two sets of parameters. The first is the sphere of human life within which the will operates. These are three: biological necessity, civil life, and works pleasing to God (section 2). Of these he grants a degree of freedom to the first and second but denies any freedom of will whatsoever to the third (section 4). The second set of parameters relates to four historical phases: man was originally created with free will and was able to sin if he so chose (and he did) (section 2). As a result, he was cast into a state in which he could not but sin. Then, as recipient of the grace of God, he vacillates between sinning and not sinning. Finally, having died and been carried to God's presence he will be entirely free of the capacity to sin (sections 2 and 6). These parameters will be familiar to nearly everyone as those famously laid out by Augustine in his *Enchiridion*.[15]

Besides these parameters that form the backdrop against which Vermigli discusses the question of free will, there are other unmistakable Augustinian influences. One has already been alluded to: like Augustine, Vermigli denies man any free will whatsoever in things pertaining to God's pleasure and requires a complete re-orientation effected from outside himself in order to please God at all (section 4). Yet once regenerated by the grace of God through the quickening power of the Holy Spirit, man now enjoys a freer will and can potentially performs actions that please God (section 24). Finally, echoing Augustine's thinking about the noble deeds of the pagans as "resplendent vices" (*splendida vitia*), Vermigli asserts that all deeds, no matter how apparently virtuous, if done outside of Christ, are actually sins (sections 14 and 15).[16]

In this way one finds an eclectic blend of Aristotelian intellectualism and Augustinian voluntarism in Vermigli's treatment of the will.[17] This is hardly surprising, seeing that

---

15. Augustine, *Enchiridion* 118, in *Nicene and Post-Nicene Fathers* (hereafter *NPNF*), edited by Philip Schaff (Grand Rapids, MI: Eerdmans, 1980 reprint), 1/3:275.

16. Augustine, *De civitate Dei* 1.12–20 (*City of God, NPNF* 1/2:29–34).

17. This assessment squares well with Luca Bashera's, who similarly finds a "fundamental eclecticism" in his analysis of Vermigli's relationship with Aristotle and scholasticism. This eclecticism was "first of all

these two thinkers combined constitute perhaps the single greatest influence on the Reformers, as they had been on the humanists as well.[18] Yet it is perhaps owing to the Aristotelian strain in Vermigli's thought that he appears at times to be ready to grant regenerate man a greater role in his sanctification than Augustine seems to do. Since, from an intellectualist position, conversion means *primarily* the rectification of a distorted mind, and furthermore, since the will quite obediently jumps to the mind's beck and call, once a person has been converted and received "the light of faith" (*lux fidei*, section 24), there is little besides either a hyperemotional state that temporarily disables proper ratiocination or sheer stubbornness of desire to keep one from behaving rightly. Accordingly, concerning the capacity of the regenerate will Vermigli concludes, "Thus our minds are, as they say, passive vis-à-vis the first transformation, or impression, of the Holy Spirit, yet after we are convinced and transformed, we are restored to be-

---

a consequence of his [Vermigli's] conviction that biblical revelation represented the only criterion of truth." See Luca Baschera, "Aristotle and Scholasticism," in *Companion to Peter Martyr Vermigli*, 159.

18. In his eclecticism Vermigli is similar to Calvin, who likewise follows an intellectualist paradigm in explaining decision-making (see *Institutes* 2.2 and Paul Helm, *John Calvin's Ideas* [New York: Oxford University Press, 2004], 135), yet recognizes the phenomenon of *akrasia* or *intemperantia*, which he says is a refusal of the will to abide by the decisions of the mind and "is not snuffed out or overcome by one's awareness of sin, but on the contrary stubbornly doubles down in the decision for wickedness that it made" (*Institutes* 2.2.23, present author's translation). One wishes this passage also explored what the implications might be for an intellectualist position given the admission that *akrasia* is a real possibility. Cf. Saarinen, *Weakness of the Will*, 9–10.

ing able to cooperate (*cooperari*) with grace and the Holy Spirit" (section 23).[19] One wishes he had gone into more depth in these passages as to the extent to which, or way in which, he means one so cooperates, but such elucidation was perhaps beyond the scope of the commentaries the passages come from. Of a piece with this cooperation is a less-than-robust view of the way one should acknowledge God's authorship in all of one's good works. Emphasis on God's authorship falls on the beginning, on conversion:

> However, those who have been born again ought never to forget that they have not acquired this freedom by their own merits, but rather by God's kindness. He refashioned them and in place of a heart of stone put a heart of flesh in them. They have their heavenly Father, not themselves, to thank for their being drawn to Christ. Unless they had been inwardly convinced in their minds through God the Father's powerful might, they would have fled from Christ no less than the others (section 23).

In stark contrast to such statements is the sentiment that caused Augustine so much grief from his Pelagian adversaries: "Give what Thou commandest, and command what Thou wilt,"[20] or Paul's declaration that the grace of

---

19. There are similar statements, e.g., "However, the paltriness of our freedom does not prevent us from cooperating with God and the Holy Spirit, making ourselves, as it were, suitable instruments" (section 24).

20. Augustine, *Confessiones* 10.29 (*Confessions*, NPNF 1/1:153).

God was more responsible for the work he did than he himself (1 Cor. 15:10).

Besides free will strictly conceived, Vermigli discusses several others matters that formed the topic of many debates between Protestants and Roman Catholics during the sixteenth century. One is the narrative about the centurion Cornelius in Acts 10. How this episode is to be interpreted is particularly important to Vermigli's denial of free will, because part and parcel of that position is the denial that one can accomplish good deeds before becoming reborn and a believer in Christ (section 10). Vermigli's response to this challenge is to maintain that faith is not a clear, cut-and-dried state, but rather a dynamic experience that undergoes development, refinement, and definition over time (section 12). Before Peter's arrival, Cornelius believed in God and was waiting for the promised Messiah, the two most important preconditions for qualifying as a believer. The only thing he lacked was knowledge of the identity of the Messiah, and this is what Peter brought (section 11).

On a related note, Vermigli must also grapple with the contention that there were righteous pagans who performed righteous deeds. As mentioned already, Vermigli flatly denies that these deeds were really righteous. Here, as often, Vermigli appeals to Augustine's *City of God* and maintains that, while these deeds resulted in beneficial results for their cities and societies, the motivation was never altruistic, and certainly not directed towards God, but rather animated by a love of praise (section 15).[21] For Ver-

---

21. Augustine, *De civitate Dei* 1.12–20 (*City of God*, NPNF 1/2:29–34).

migli, whatever deed is driven by what the Greeks called φιλαυτία (love of self) is in no way directed to God and can only be evil (section 19). He enumerates five characteristics required of a work in order for it to be called truly good. The first is that the doer must be animated by God's Spirit; the second, that faith must be present; the third is that it must be done for God's glory, not one's own or anything else; the fourth is that grace and mercy must be present throughout by the presence of Christ; the fifth is that God must be recognized as the ultimate cause (section 19). These characteristics being an impossibility to both ancient pagans and contemporary unbelievers, the inescapable conclusion is that their deeds were not, theologically speaking, good.

Consequently, lest God appear to condemn souls to eternal punishment without due cause, Vermigli must point out that it is not so much sin that condemns a person as sinfulness. That is, Vermigli must argue that man's innate concupiscence is a sin. To do so, he deploys an interesting argument. Picking up Paul's statement that the wages of sin is death (Romans 6:23), he points out that people die only because they are sinful. Since death is the result and product of sin, the fact that people die is proof of their sinfulness. The case of infants is now instructive. They neither have actual sins, that is, volitional sins, because they have not lived long enough to accrue them; nor, in the case of infants who have been baptized, do they suffer from the guilt of original sin.[22] Yet they die. Therefore, either God is unrighteous or they die because their

---

22. This argument certainly has implications for Vermigli's doctrine of baptism. See section 26.

inborn propensity to sin is itself a sin (section 26). The same holds for the initial promptings to sin. Though they have not yet and may never be actually realized in action, they are still sins (section 27).

The language of the *Common Places* can at times cause confusion because of its nature as a set of excerpts. Hitherto, Vermigli has been defending the position that man has no free will, especially in matters pertaining to God and salvation. However, the section on free will concludes with an excerpt from Vermigli's commentary on 1 Corinthians where he argues that man does indeed have free will. But the two different goals he had in each work explains the difference of language. In the former he is explaining why we do not have the capacity to choose the things of God and contribute to our justification. Now in the latter he is explaining how our inability to will the things of God does not mean that violence is done to our will. The important distinction is that while we sin *necessarily*, we do not sin under coercion. We cannot choose the things of God precisely because we will the opposite (section 35; cf. section 5).

Vermigli makes this distinction in the context of his discussion of why God's foreknowledge and providence is compatible with our free will. The evil we choose we choose freely, Vermigli explains, and God foresees not simply our acting, but our willing as well (section 35). As he categorically states, "The human will never realizes anything but what God foreknows and wills it to realize" (section 35). Interestingly, the foil Vermigli chooses to use in this discussion is none other than the great Roman orator and hero of the humanists, Marcus Tullius Cicero. Responding to a position found partly in the orator's *On the Nature of the Gods* and partly in his *On Divination*,[23] Vermigli castigates him for preferring to limit, or even do away with, divine foreknowledge than to sacrifice the free operation of the human will.

This critical stance toward Cicero should, however, not be taken as a rejection on Vermigli's part of the program or ideals of the humanism of his Italian compatriots. First of all, Vermigli had good precedent, as he himself acknowledges, in Augustine's critical attitude towards the Roman. Besides this, there was a long tradition within Italian humanism of taking Cicero to task on various issues, the most famous being Petrarch's letter to Cicero in which he expresses his substantial disappointment that Cicero had been enticed by considerations of glory and fame to give up a life of quiet philosophical contemplation and get involved in the stormy (and ultimately fatal) politics of civil war.[24] Indeed, the fact that Vermigli chose to discuss this question in conversation with Cicero and not some other more philosophical or Scholastic author is probably a sign of abiding humanist attitudes in Vermigli as well as humanist interests on the part of his readership, rather than any rejection of that program. Nor did Vermigli's rejection of free will in man's salvation suggest any real departure from humanism, as several humanists, most notably Lorenzo Valla, had already expressed serious

---

23. See section 34, footnote 8 of the translation for a rough disambiguation of the two works.

24. Petrarch, *Fam.* 14.3, translation in Mario Emilio Cosenza, *Petrarch's Letters to Classical Authors* (Chicago: University of Chicago Press, 1910), 1–3.

misgivings about the idea of free will and its compatibility with the doctrine of grace.[25]

After Vermigli's treatment of the compatibility of God's foreknowledge with man's free will, there follows the chapter on the Law, extracted from various of his commentaries. Here Vermigli attempts to discuss the Law and define what it is, interestingly, on the basis of traditional Aristotelian definition, that is, according to the four causes. Thus the Law's formal cause is spirit, while its final cause, or end, is salvation. God himself is the efficient cause, while its material cause is no less than the will and character of God himself, since what God commands us to do or be is what He himself already is and practices. In light of the influence Aristotle continued to exert on the humanists and Reformers (despite all their criticism of the Stagirite), as well as Vermigli's use of Aristotle in his discussion of man's will as articulated above, this incorporation of Aristotelian theory into his treatment of the Law is anything but surprising. Besides, the four-cause theory was the standard way of defining a thing well into the early modern period. Yet it also suggests Vermigli had realist assumptions and commitments in his thinking despite the nominalism that has often been seen in other Reformers.[26]

---

25. See, for example, Lorenzo Valla, *On Free Will* (*De libero arbitrio*), trans. Charles Trinkaus, in Ernst Cassirer et al., *The Renaissance Philosophy of Man* (Chicago: University of Chicago Press, 1948).

26. Indeed, John Patrick Donnelly, *Calvinism and Scholasticism in Vermigli's Doctrine of Man and Grace* (Leiden: Brill, 1976), 202–7, has argued that Vermigli's Thomism exerted a great influence on other Reformers, particularly Zanchi and Beza, and was a key factor in the rise of Protestant scholasticism.

It is also a good example of moments when Vermigli's exegesis can become almost devotional. Unpacking the idea that the material cause is equivalent to God's will and character, Vermigli uses the example of love and explains that God "desires us to be participants in himself" (*On the Law*, section 1), thus reminding the reader that love of God must be the Christian's most basic motivation and that, as Paul expressed it, without love we are nothing (1 Cor. 13:2).

Vermigli then goes on to explain how the Manicheans are in error when they say the Law is evil. The Law was the instrument through which death entered, but that was because of our sin, not because of the Law *per se*. The Law merely points out sin and error; it doesn't create it. Also, the Law seems odious to us because it calls us back from the sin we want to engage in and constrains us when we would rather do whatever we please. He ends the section by describing how God can change us so that, in our mind (*mens*) at least, we love the Law (section 2). He next goes on to castigate the Pelagians (section 3). Man, he says, on his own cannot fulfill the Law. If he could, there would be no need for Christ's death. He then briefly discusses the uses of the Law and gives a very traditional account of the threefold use of the law (conviction, civil order, guidance in sanctification).

At first sight it might seem that Vermigli is engaging in the straw man fallacy, since both the Manichaeans and Pelagians were ancient heretics whose false ideas Augustine had done much to lay to rest. Upon reflection, though, such a refutation of Manichaean and Pelagian doctrines was relevant and topical. The mantra of the *via moderna*, "God does not deny his grace to those who do what lies in them" (*facientibus quod in se est Deus non denegat gratiam suam*), popularized by Gabriel Biel and forming the lining of Thomas à Kempis's *Imitation of Christ*, was often felt to be too close to Pelagian assumptions for the Reformers' comfort (despite the popularity, especially in Reformation Zürich, of the latter work),[27] while various groups within what is traditionally labeled "The Radical Reformation"— groups often referred to as libertines, antinomians, and, mockingly, catabaptists by the mainline Reformers—were thought to go so far in their critical attitude to the Law and its salutary benefits as to elicit a charge of Manichaeism on more than one occasion. Thus, while Vermigli nowhere in these two chapters explicitly states that these groups are in his crosshairs, it is no surprise that these passages in particular were excerpted by his editor to be included in the *Common Places*.

Finally, the chapter ends with a selection of guidelines taken from multiple commentaries of Vermigli and meant to show how one should apply the Law in cases where God's Word appears to give two commands that are mutually exclusive. His two rules of thumb are that

---

27. For the *via moderna* and Gabriel Biel, see Alister McGrath, *Historical Theology: An Introduction to the History of Christian Thought*, 2nd ed. (Chichester: Wiley-Blackwell, 2013), 118–20. According to McGrath, thinkers of this school evaded the charge of Pelagianism by affirming that man's works *per se* were worthless, but that God by a merciful *acceptation* deigned to regard them as valuable, like lead coins plated in gold. For *via moderna* ideas in Thomas à Kempis, see his *Imitatio Christi* I.7 and IV.7, where doing what lies within one's power (*facere quod in se est*) plays a crucial role. Regarding the popularity of the *Imitation of Christ* in Reformation Zürich, one can point to the German translation made of it by Leo Jud (*Nachvolgung Christi* [Zürich: Augustin Friess, 1539]).

when this happens, one should either obey the latter or the more important one. He then proceeds to explain the application of these rules with concrete examples (sections 6 and 7). One should note that Chapter Three is short (approximately one-fourth the length of the chapter on free will), and is so because it serves as an introduction to the following chapters of the *Common Places* where Vermigli discusses each item of the Decalogue individually and at great length.

About the Translation and Sources

The base text I used for the translation was the first edition entitled *Petri Martyris Vermilii Florentini praestantissimi nostra aetate theologi Loci Communes*, printed in London in 1576 by John Kyngston, and prepared by Robert Masson,[28] who composed the prefatory letter. This work was translated into English seven years later in 1583 by Anthony Marten and printed by H. Denham and H. Middleton under the title *The Common places of the most famous and renowned Divine Doctor Peter Martyr*. It is a very close and literal translation of the 1576 Latin edition, so its value in resolving textual problems, of which there are not a few, is minimal (although Marten's translation does correct some typos, mostly those involving section numbers).

In resolving the handful of textual problems that arose in the course of translating I had recourse to the first editions of the commentaries from which this portion of the *Common Places* was taken. Their bibliographical information can be found in the first footnote of each section

---

28. For information on Masson, see above footnote 2.

that has been drawn from them. Any subsequent reference to them, especially when pertaining to textual variants, uses the shorthand of the Bible book in question and the date of publication (using place of publication along with the date, given the fact that many of these commentaries were published numerous times at the same press, could give rise to confusion). So, the shorthand reference to his commentary on Romans is *Romans 1558*. I also consulted subsequent editions of the *Common Places* themselves, although not all.[29] The ones I did consult, in addition of course to the London 1576, were the Zürich edition of 1580 and the Heidelberg edition of 1603. These three editions, together with the first editions of the commentaries that supplied this portion of the work in the first place, were sufficient to disentangle the few discrepancies that arose during translation. The shorthand reference to an edition of the *Loci* will be the place of publication followed by the year. So, a reference to the Heidelberg edition of 1603 will be *Heidelberg 1603*. This way of proceeding also shed some light on the practice of the various editors. The London editor preferred to reproduce the errors found in the original commentaries (while introducing some of his own as well), while later editors preferred to correct both sets of errors, either by referring back to the original commentaries or using their own ingenuity or common sense (whatever the case may be).

---

29. For more information on the fourteen editions of the *Loci* that appeared between 1576 and 1656, see McClelland, "Literary History," in *Companion to Peter Martyr Vermigli*, 479–94; see also John Patrick Donnelly, SJ, Robert Kingdon, and Marvin Anderson, *A Bibliography of the Works of Peter Martyr Vermigli* (Ann Arbor, MI: Edwards Brothers, 1990), 98–126.

The aim of the present translation was to improve upon Marten not simply by offering a more up-to-date version, but one which aimed at being less Latinate and more idiomatically English in its style. It also presents a different construal of several passages where the present translator believes Marten simply erred and misread the Latin (which translators are apt to do). Finally, it aimed at providing a more user-friendly format. The original Latin text has no paragraph divisions and uses Roman numerals to set off extended sections within which several topics are discussed. Accordingly, what the reader sees is a more or less continuous text with few breaks and only marginal summaries (taken directly from the original commentaries) to help navigate. I have therefore added chapter numbers and titles while preserving the original section numbers, but included these in square brackets so that the reader would know they originate with the translator, not with Vermigli.

Several people provided me with indispensable help in the preparation of the present volume. I am especially grateful to Dr. Kirk Summers of the University of Alabama, who invited me to participate in this project and who helped me in countless ways from beginning to end; to Dr. Timothy Edwards of New Saint Andrews College for his consummate expertise in Hebrew, which enabled me to disentangle the way Vermigli used the Hebrew Bible and rabbinic commentaries; and to Laura Grace Alexander of The Geneva School, who was extremely helpful in the citations to the myriad of names and works Vermigli refers to in the course of his exegesis. Finally, special thanks goes to my wife who bore with patience my frequent absence to work on this translation.

PETER MARTYR VERMIGLI: SECOND PART OF THE COMMON PLACES

SECOND CHAPTER

On free will

[CHAPTER 1: FREE WILL]

1. It will now be worthwhile to discuss briefly the freedom of our will. For the moment we shall consider what degree of freedom has been left to us by the innate depravity resulting from original sin, especially since we are told to attribute completely to the grace of God whatever upright action we perform.

While the term *free will* does not occur in Scripture, the idea itself should not be considered fabricated or made up. The Greeks call it αὐτεξούσιον, which means *in one's own power* or *under one's own control*. Latin-speakers express the same idea when they say *arbitrii libertas*, that is, *freedom of will*. *Free* means that which does not follow the will of another, but its own, while *will* is thought to consist in our following, as we deem fit, the decisions we arrived at by reason. Accordingly, the will is free when it embraces, as it likes,[1] those decisions which are approved by the cognitive part of the mind. Thus, the nature of free will, while most evident in volition, has its roots in reason, and

---

1. In saying *free* and *as it likes*, Vermigli is making use of an etymological argument, since in Latin the former is *libera* and the latter is *prout libuerit*.

those who wish to use this faculty correctly must above all see to it that there occurs no error in their reasoning. Error usually occurs in two ways: we either fail to see what is just and unjust in the performance of our actions; or, if we see it, we err in our examination of the reasons that are brought forward for either side, for desire in us nearly always favors the weaker argument. This is why the stronger and better position is often dismissed and rejected. We see this sometimes happening in debates: those who wish to defend the weaker side tend to adorn it with every sort of rhetorical flourish and embellishment so that the audience will be attracted to the polish and allure and not weigh the strength and soundness of the reasoning.

Furthermore, one should recognize that deliberation[2] does not address just any issue, but only those issues that are called *performative* (πρακτικαί), that is, actions to be performed by us. Not everything that we pursue or reject requires deliberation. Some things are so clearly and undoubtedly good that it is enough for them to be proposed, for they are immediately either chosen or rejected, such as happiness, unhappiness, life, death, and whatever else is in this class. Other things are less clear, or rather occupy middle ground. It is about these that people tend to deliberate. Everybody admits without hesitation that God is to be worshiped. However, *how* he is to be worshiped and in what ceremonies is the subject of the greatest controversy. Everybody knows that it is expedient for people to come together in cities and cultivate community with each other, but by what laws they are to be governed and what form of government they should use are questions

---

2. I.e., deliberation as the exercise and activity of the human will.

that often give rise to deep uncertainty. It is in these and similar questions that free will applies.

2. I define free will as follows: it is the faculty by which we either espouse or reject, as we like, those decisions that have been made by reason. Now, it cannot be laid out in one simple response whether or not men have such a faculty, or how it operates in them. It is first necessary to determine man's state and condition. At least four different states are found in man: one state, and far different, was Adam's when he was created in the beginning. There was another after he fell. This is the current state of his entire progeny. Further, those who have been reborn in Christ enjoy a much better state than those who live outside of Christ. Yet we are going to enjoy the happiest and freest of states when we put off this mortal body. We will therefore respond to the proposed question in the context of these four conditions.

[CHAPTER 2:
THE STATES OF THE WILL]

We must believe that from the first moment of his creation Adam was free. Before this idea can be fleshed out, a distinction must be made among three types of actions that take place in us. Of these actions some are natural, as being sick, being healthy, being nourished, digesting food, and other such things. In these actions, while the first man enjoyed a much more blessed existence than we do at present, he was still subject to a kind of necessity, for he had to eat and be nourished and consume food, yet he was exempt from all the adversities that could cause death. There are other actions that, from a civil or moral perspective, are either just or unjust. The third type is those actions that are pleasing and gratifying to God.

As far as all of these types are concerned, man was from the beginning created free, since he was made in the image of God, for whom nothing is more fitting than true and genuine freedom. Also, it is written about him, "God crowned him with glory and honor" [Psalm 8:5], and "though he was honored, he did not understand" [Psalm 48:21]. Now, what honor can there be when there is no freedom? Finally, God put what he had created under man's control. If he had been created a slave to his passions and desires, he could certainly have never exercised true dominion over them in right reason. However, since Scripture leaves us in the dark concerning what that state was, nothing can be determined with certainty. In his *On Rebuke and Grace* Augustine says, "The aid of God's grace was conferred on Adam, yet such was the aid that he could relinquish it, when he wished, and could remain in it, if he wished, yet it could not bring about his wishing."[1]

On this score, Augustine goes so far as to set the grace that we now possess through Christ above the grace that Adam had in paradise, for now by the grace of Christ we not only persevere, provided we are willing, but, as Paul says, thanks to it, we also possess both the willing and its accomplishment, since the heart of believers is changed and they are transformed from those who do not will into those who do; by contrast, in the first man, the capacity to will depended on his will alone and was not brought about in him by God's grace. Explaining why God bestowed free will on Adam when he was first created, Augustine says in book two of *On Free Will* that God had ordained to demonstrate his goodness and justice towards him. He intended to show his goodness towards him if he acted rightly, a thing of course he could not have done unless he had been free; if, on the other hand, he acted shamefully and badly, God intended to exercise the severity of his justice towards him. As it turned out, in his freedom

---

1. Augustine, *De correptione et gratia* 31 (*On Rebuke and Grace*, NPNF 1/5:484).

he fell miserably.[2] Just as Christ tells how a man coming down from Jerusalem to Jericho came upon robbers and was terribly beaten by them, likewise Adam was left in a half-dead and desperate state, not only losing his garment and ornaments of distinction, but receiving many wounds as well.

3. Consequently, we assert that, as far as the second state is concerned, since we are alienated from Christ, we retain very little freedom, for we are subject to the necessities of nature and, whether we wish it or not, are afflicted by diseases and finally subdued by death. There is, however, a degree of freedom, as far as civil and moral actions are concerned, as these fall within natural knowledge and do not exceed the powers of our will, even though in the case of these actions, too, people experience considerable distress because their mad desires work against moral uprightness. Enticements and delights constantly batter our senses. These are compounded by wicked persuaders. Satan also constantly prods and pushes. Envying humanity's advantages and aware that civilization is held together by moral actions, he is eager to overturn them by all means.

And yet the many good laws issued by Lycurgus, Solon, Numa, and others show that man's powers are quite efficacious in this civil sphere, at least as far as his judgment is concerned. Similarly, Paul says to the Romans, "Do you think, O man, that you will escape God's judgment, when you commit the same acts that you judge?" [Rom. 2:3]. There are, moreover, two considerations in this sphere that must not be overlooked. The first is that God makes full

2. Vermigli appears to be paraphrasing Augustine, *De libero arbitrio* 2.204–5.

use of men's will for the purposes that he himself ordains. The second, which follows from the previous one, is that the outcomes aimed at by those engaged in civil affairs are not realized, for often entirely different outcomes come about than they would have ever imagined. This frequently caused pagans a great deal of distress. Pompey, Cato, and Cicero thought they had devised outstanding courses of action, but when they came to nothing, nothing was left to their devisers but despair. Foiled in their plans, they blamed the entire failure on fortune and chance.

But Jeremiah declares that the issue of actions and the outcome of plans are in God's hands, when he says, "The way of man is not his own, nor is it in the power of a man to direct his steps" [10:23]. The Jews interpret this passage as relating to Nebuchadnezzar. They say that he set out to wage war against the Ammonites, not against the Jews, as is related in Ezekiel 21 [vv. 20–21]. However, when he came to where two ways met, he began to deliberate, consulted entrails, teraphim, and lots by the gleam of a sword,[3] and having gained guidance in this way, dis-

---

3. In the reading "lots by the gleam of the sword" in Ezekiel 21:21 (v. 26 in the Hebrew Bible), one gets insight into Vermigli's use of Hebrew and the rabbinic tradition in studying the Bible. For the Masoretic לקלק םיצחב, the Vulgate reads "mixing up arrows" (*commiscens sagittas*), while the LXX reads, evidently, "tossing up a staff" (τοῦ ἀναβράσαι ῥάβδον). It is customarily rendered in English translations as "shaking arrows." The fact that Vermigli interprets it as taking "lots by the gleam of a sword" (*sortes ex fulgore gladii*) betrays his use of the thirteenth-century Provençal Jewish Rabbi David Kimhi, who mentions this divinatory practice in his commentary on Ezekiel. See David b. Joseph Kimhi, "Commentary on Ezekiel," in תולודג תוארקמ רפס יחזקאל :רתכה [Mikra'ot Gedolot 'Haketer': A Revised and Scientific of 'Mikra'ot Gedolot,' Based on the Aleppo Codex and Early

regarded the Ammonites, invaded Judaea, and laid siege to Jerusalem.

These two ideas, that God is the author of plans and gives what outcome he wants to actions, are not lost on the godly. Accordingly, they do not make any decisions touching upon themselves without adding the proviso "if God wishes," a thing James teaches should be done. Similarly, in his letter to the Romans, Paul says that he desires to have a favorable journey to them, yet according to God's will [Rom. 1:10]. For this reason, if matters turn out otherwise than they hoped, they have consolation, knowing that God their excellent Father makes better provisions for his kingdom and their own welfare than they themselves could have done. They always have on their lips what David sang, "Unless the LORD builds the house, those who build it have labored in vain" [Psalm 127:1]. They are therefore concerned to adapt their plans to God's Word. They commit the outcome to God, and thus they live unperturbed from every direction.

4. However, since men are alienated from God, they have no freedom when it comes to actions that are to be pleasing and approved before him. Hence Augustine says in his *Enchiridion*, that man destroyed both himself and his free will by misusing his free will, for sin won the contest and reduced man to servitude.[4] I know that there are some who interpret Augustine's statement as saying Adam

---

Medieval MSS: Ezekiel], ed. Menachem Cohen (Ramat-Gan: Bar Ilan University, 2000), 137–38. For more on Vermigli's activity in Hebraic studies, see Max Engammare, "Humanism, Hebraism, and Scriptural Hermeneutics," in *Companion to Peter Martyr Vermigli*, 161–74.

4. Augustine, *Enchiridion* 30 (*NPNF* 1/3:247).

lost free will as far as grace and glory are concerned, but not as concerns his nature. I am not, to be sure, going to take great pains here to deny that reason and will—which are parts of our nature—have been left to man after the Fall; but they themselves cannot deny that that same nature is crippled and wounded. This even the teacher of the *Sentences* asserts in book two, distinction twenty-five.[5] He says that now after the Fall man is in the position where he can sin and, what is more, cannot not sin. And even if Augustine and others had not made this assertion, a compelling argument could demonstrate it: godly actions result from two sources, knowledge and appetite. Regarding knowledge Paul says, "The natural man does not comprehend the things that belong to the spirit of God; indeed, he is not even able, since they are foolishness to him" [1 Cor. 2:13]. Now, if we do not perceive[6] what we are to do and what is pleasing to God, how indeed are we able to carry it out in action?

Furthermore, it is clear from Genesis 6 how our appetite and knowledge are related to them (i.e., the things of the spirit of God). God says, "My spirit will not contend with man forever, because he is flesh" [Gen. 6:3]; and a little later, "God saw that great was men's wickedness and everything produced in the thoughts of his heart aimed at only evil all his days" [Gen. 6:5]; and in chapter 8: "What is produced by the heart of man is evil right from his infancy" [Gen. 8:21]. It is God himself who says these things,

---

5. Peter Lombard, *Sentences* 2.25.

6. Vermigli's language strengthens his argument. In saying "if we do not perceive," he uses the word *cognoscimus*, which recalls the "knowledge," *cognitio*, mentioned just above.

and on the topic of our powers we are to believe nobody more than our Potter, whenever he bears testimony about his handiwork. In Jeremiah 18, the people say, "We will follow our thoughts" [v. 12]. Commenting on this passage Jerome writes, "Therefore, without God's grace, where is the power of free will and the judgment of one's own volition, seeing that following one's own thoughts and carrying out the will of a depraved heart is an outrageous offense against God?"[7] Christ teaches us in John that we are subject to servitude: "He who commits sin is a slave to sin" [John 8:34]. Therefore, since we commit many sins and bear sin innately from our mother's womb, we must necessarily admit that we are slaves. But we will truly be free if the Son sets us free; otherwise, we are slaves in the bitterest of slaveries. For this reason Paul said he was sold under sin [Rom. 7:14]—so sold as to confess that nothing good inhabited his flesh—and did what he did not want and what he hated [Rom. 7:18–19]; he sensed another law in his limbs, opposing the law of his mind and taking him captive to the law of sin [Rom. 7:23]. To the Galatians he says the flesh fights against the spirit and the spirit against the flesh, so that we do not do what we want [Gal. 5:17].

If this is true in the case of so great an apostle and in the case of holy individuals born again through Christ, what is one to think of the ungodly who do not belong to Christ? They cannot approach him unless they are drawn. Christ says, "Nobody can come to me, unless my Father draws him" [John 6:44]. Augustine makes the point that a person who wants to come beforehand of his own volition

---

7. Jerome, *Commentarii in Jeremiam Prophetam* 4.18.11–13 (*PL* 24:797B).

is not *drawn*, but *led*. Therefore, if we have to be *drawn* to Christ, we do not wish it beforehand, which is a very serious sin. And we do not wish, because the wisdom of the flesh is enmity against God, for it is not subject to the law of God; indeed, it is not even able to be subject [Rom. 8:7]. All who have not been liberated through Christ live under the law and, as Paul adds in Galatians, under a curse [3:10]. This would not be true if they were able to obey God's law, since only those who transgress the law become liable to a curse. Moreover, Paul clearly states, "It is not of the one who wills or runs, but of God who has mercy" [Rom. 9:16]. Our salvation is *his* work, not our ability's. He is the one who works in us both the will and its accomplishment [Phil. 2:13]. Before he brings that about, if he has any interaction with us either through the law or through the teaching of his Word, it is with stones that he has interaction. Our hearts are stone, unless Christ transforms them into flesh. In Ezekiel he promises that he will do this, and that he will cause us to walk in his precepts [11:12].

And clearly if we were able to live justly and rightly without grace, we would also be able to be justified by our works, an idea that is flatly rejected by both Paul and all of Scripture. Jeremiah says, "Turn me, LORD, and I will be turned" [Jer. 31:18]. David says, "Create in me a clean heart, God" [Psalm 51:10]. From chapter 29 of Deuteronomy we realize that this is not done in everybody's case, where it is written, "The LORD did not give you all eyes to see or an ear to hear or a heart to understand" [v. 4]. In chapter 30, God promises to circumcise their hearts and the hearts of their seed so that they can walk in his precepts [v. 6]. He both begins and completes our salvation.

Paul says to the Philippians, "I expect that he who began [a good work]⁸ in you will see it through to the day of Christ" [Phil. 1:6]. Realizing this, holy men pray with David, "Incline my heart to your statutes" [Psalm 119:36], and with Solomon, "May the LORD incline our hearts so that we walk in His ways" [1 Kings 8:58], and with Paul to the Thessalonians, "May God direct your hearts in patience and anticipation of Christ" [2 Thess. 3:5]. Similarly, Solomon says in Proverbs, "The heart of a king is in God's hand; he will direct it wherever he wishes" [Prov. 21:1]. These passages are sufficient to show that our turning to him and doing good are the work of God.

---

8. These words are omitted in Vermigli's quotation.

[CHAPTER 3:
NECESSITY AND COERCION
DISTINGUISHED]

5. At this point certain individuals retort, bringing up the commandments in Scripture which appear to imply that keeping what is commanded is within our power. Isaiah says, "If you wish and hearken to me, you will eat the good things of the land" [Isaiah 1:19]. Likewise, the LORD often commands us to turn to him: "Turn to me. I do not desire the death of a sinner, but prefer that he turn and live" [Ezek. 18:23], and when publishing the law he said that he held forth life and death, blessing and curse. Countless other passages could be cited, but here we should note that, while these commandments are made to men, we are nowhere taught that they can be carried out by any individual's own strength. And neither is it right to infer the greatness of our strength on the basis of the commands of God's law, as though we were able to perform on our own accord all that God's law commands. On the contrary, they should rather cause us to assess our weakness and realize, when we see the perfection and greatness of God's commandments exceed

our strength by an incalculable margin, that there is some other purpose for the law than our fulfilling it.

That purpose Paul shows to be manifold. He says, "Through the law comes recognition of sin" [Rom. 3:20] and adds that the law was passed in order for the number of transgressions to increase. In this way the law proves to be a pedagogue,[1] to bring men to Christ, so that when they themselves get overwhelmed by the weight of the commandments and the enormity of their sins, they can recognize that their salvation lies in God's mercy and Christ's redemption. For as soon as we realize our inability and unworthiness, we immediately begin to beg God to forgive our sins through Christ, to provide us with the aid of his Holy Spirit, and for us to desire to desire his will. "Give what You command, and command what You wish," says Augustine.[2] Furthermore, another use of the law is for us to see what goal we should be striving towards. It is even possible for people to conform to the law if by God's grace a fledgling obedience is granted. Finally, seeing that it is not granted to us in this life to be able to satisfy the law flawlessly, we shall nevertheless fully gain this in the next life, when we have thrown off all of this corruption.[3]

However, God should not be accused of unfairness on this account, as it is not his fault that his requirements

---

1. In antiquity, the *pedagogue* was typically a slave tasked with taking care of the master's children and, in particular, escorting them to and from school.

2. Augustine, *Confessiones* 10.29 (*Confessions*, NPNF 1/1:153).

3. For a focused discussion by Vermigli of the law, see *On the Law* below.

cannot be met. But neither can any of us be excused, seeing that we willfully and desirously violate the law set before us. A body of legislation that might correspond as closely as possible with our nature (as it was originally designed) was passed; the image of God could not have been expressed more clearly or effectively in any other way. Now, if we cannot fulfill the law because of sin, we at least see how we ought to be.

6. The frequently adduced statement that only that which results from deliberate decision should be considered a sin ought to be taken, as Augustine interprets it, as pertaining to the class of sin that is not the penalty of sin. After all, original guilt is neither voluntary nor undertaken by deliberate decision. But you will say, "This being the case, we are evidently necessarily stuck in sin." Indeed, I would not deny that. However, this necessity is not the kind that entails coercion. God is necessarily good and cannot in any way sin; yet he is not forcibly coerced to be good. In *City of God* Augustine makes the elegant comment, "As for God himself, surely one should not say he does not have free will because he is unable to sin?"[4] In *On Faith, to Emperor Gratian*, Ambrose attests to God's freedom when he says, "One and the same Spirit performs everything, distributing to everything as he wishes, according to the discretion of his free will, not in submission to necessity."[5]

---

4. Augustine, *De civitate Dei* 22.30 (*City of God*, NPNF 1/2:510).

5. Ambrose, *De fide ad Gratianum* 2.48 [chapter 6, not chapter 3, as Vermigli records] (*Exposition of the Christian Faith*, NPNF 2/10:229).

In these Fathers' statements free will is taken as opposed to force and coercion, and not in the sense of being equally disposed in either direction. Consequently, in his homily *De filio prodigo*, which he wrote to Damasus, Jerome wrote differently about free will because he understood it differently. He says, "God is the only one whom sin does not and cannot characterize. Everything else, since it has free will, can be turned in either direction."[6] Not being able to sin also characterizes the blessed spirits and angels, since their felicity is already confirmed. Accordingly, in *City of God*, Augustine says, "Just as the first immortality, which Adam lost by his sin, was the *ability* not to die, so the first free will was the *ability* not to sin, whereas the last will be the *inability* to sin."[7] Be that as it may, the blessed spirits and angels still have a certain kind of freedom, not in that they can be turned in either direction, but in that, while they act necessarily, they are not coerced or forcibly acted upon.[8] For just as some truths are so obvious that the mind cannot but give its assent to them, in the same way, when God's presence is revealed and made apparent, so great is his goodness that the saints are unable to withdraw from it. In this way, although we

---

6. The reference is actually to Letter 21 in Jerome's correspondence. See *CSEL* 54:139. Vermigli's belief that the statement came from a homily is possibly due to the occurrence of this very statement in Peter Lombard's *Sentences* (2.25), where it is so described.

7. Augustine, *De civitate Dei* 22.30 (*City of God, NPNF* 1/2:510).

8. One wishes Vermigli had addressed the issue of why, as commonly held in the Christian tradition, Lucifer fell, if being in God's presence commands naturally and necessarily, yet not coercively, this sort of reaction.

necessarily sin before being reborn in Christ, the rights of our will are still not violated, since whatever we do, we do both willingly and driven by some motivation.

Nor should we be considered no different than the brute beasts. They are impelled by a kind of judgment, just not a free one; humans, on the other hand, even those not yet reborn, still retain a good deal of freedom, as we have said, as far as civil and moral actions are concerned. Secondly, they have a choice between the actual sins they necessarily abide in, so as to choose this and reject that, although they are unable to reach the things that are pleasing to God. These traits do not characterize brute beasts. On the contrary, these are too much driven by natural force to be able to do anything with any degree of freedom. People can be referred to as free as far as concerns either coercion, sin, or misery. The first freedom, from coercion, is given to all people. However, all who have not yet come to Christ are in every way subject to sin and misery. Later we will discuss in what way people who have been reborn are subject to sin and misery while they live on this earth; in the meantime, the idea that the will is not coerced to sin by this necessity that we posit should be a settled point [section 23–24].

7. But to lay out this entire question with greater clarity, it must be well established beforehand what the terms *free, violent,* and *spontaneous* mean. We call *free* that which, when two or more options have been proposed, is able to choose what it wants according to its pleasure. This is the reason we flatly deny the will of unregenerate individuals to be free, since it cannot choose the things that have to do with salvation. That which is moved by an outside source and does not itself contribute to that

movement, but on the contrary fights against it, is *violent*, as when a stone is thrown into the air. That which has an inner force and is inclined towards the motion it is driven in is called *spontaneous*. It is thus apparent that the spontaneous and the necessary are not mutually exclusive, since they can be combined, as is clear in the case of our will which necessarily espouses happiness, yet does so gladly and of its own accord. Moreover, the will can never be coerced into willing what it does not will. Augustine in fact thinks the idea of willing what you do not will to be as absurd as if you were to say something can be hot without heat.

However, the necessity by which the ungodly are said to sin is not so absolute and perfect as to resist alteration. For upon the approach of the Spirit and grace of Christ it at once breaks apart. For this reason Augustine says that *being able* to have faith is a matter of nature, though *having it* is entirely a matter of grace, since that potential or capability does not issue forth in action, unless grace is divinely bestowed. On this point—that the ability is innate—Augustine and Pelagius were agreed. But Augustine added that living well and rightly must be ascribed to grace alone, an assertion that Pelagius would not accept. For my part, I think that this *power of nature* requires distinction. If they mean that our nature has been so created by God that faith, hope, and love do not conflict with it (provided these are granted by God), but rather complete, perfect, and adorn it, I grant that what they say is true. But if they want *the power of nature* to mean some capacity it possesses by which it can appropriate to itself these qualities, I absolutely do not assent, for it is an ungodly and damnable statement. We therefore say that man's will does relate to both good and evil, but in different ways. While it can espouse evil on its own accord, it cannot espouse good, unless it is restored by God's grace.

[CHAPTER 4:
A CRITIQUE OF CONGRUOUS
AND CONDIGN MERIT]

Even pagan authors (compelled by the truth) sometimes taught that a certain divine inspiration was necessary in order to perform the things that are truly good. In book one of the *Ethics* Aristotle says, "If there is any gift of god, it must be considered to be blessedness,"[1] and defines *blessedness* as nothing other than an excellent act issuing from the foremost faculty of our mind through the preeminent virtue.[2] Similarly, Plato admits in a certain passage that virtues are produced in men by an inspiration of divine

---

1. Aristotle, *Nicomachean Ethics* 1.9 (1099b11–13).

2. Vermigli is referring to Aristotle's famous definition of happiness (εὐδαιμονία): τὸ ἀνθρώπινον ἀγαθὸν ψυχῆς ἐνέργεια γίνεται κατ᾽ ἀρετήν, εἰ δὲ πλείους αἱ ἀρεταί, κατὰ τὴν ἀρίστην καὶ τελειοτάτην ("What the good is for a human turns out to be the excellent activity of the soul; and if there are several kinds of excellences, [then activity] in the best and most complete one") (*Nicomachean Ethics* 1098a16–18).

power.[3] Even Scholastic theologians—those at least who had a bit more sense—admitted that for every good work God's grace was required in order to assist human strength. Since that time, they have in some way or another forgotten themselves and maintain that an unregenerate individual is able to perform some good acts that are pleasing to God and merit Christ's grace "on the basis of congruity" (*de congruo*), to use their language.

8. They call *congruous* that which we might call *fair and good*, that is, when strictness and severity of justice are relaxed; by *condign* they mean that which is owed on the basis of strict justice. But those who first conjured up these terms did not realize that admirable civil actions are still sins from God's perspective, however much they have the appearance of good to men, as Augustine incontrovertibly proves.[4] It was stated above, nor will it put me out to repeat it now: before we are turned to God, we are by nature children of wrath. John says, "The one who does not believe in the Son of God does not have eternal life, but instead the wrath of God hangs over him" (John 3:36). What can God's enemies and opponents offer to him that would be pleasing to him? Paul says to the Ephesians that before we came to Christ we were dead

---

3. Plato speaks in the singular, not the plural: θείᾳ μοίρᾳ ἡμῖν φαίνεται παραγιγνομένη ἡ ἀρετὴ οἷς ἂν παργίγνηται (*Meno* 100b2–4). Since Vermigli's time, this statement concluding the *Meno* has been read as another instance of Socratic *aporia* whereby Socrates is not saying much more than that he has no idea where ἀρετή comes from. Cf. Mark Reuter, "Is Goodness Really a Gift from God?" *Classical Association of Canada* 55, no. 1/2 (Spring/Summer 2001): 77.

4. Cf. Augustine, *De civitate Dei* 19.25 (*City of God*, NPNF 1/2:418–19).

in our trespasses and sins [Eph. 2:1]. The dead have no sensation, so they are unable to do anything that would bring them back to life.

Addressing the Philippians, Paul considered everything that he had accomplished before being turned to Christ to be loss and excrement—so far was he from placing any modicum of merit in what he had done [Phil. 3:8]. In the first chapter of Isaiah, God avows that he abhors, detests, and deems abominable the offerings the Jews were bringing without faith and true godliness (Isaiah 1:11). The same prophet likens all our acts of righteousness to menstrual rags (Isaiah 64:6). Our Savior says, "I am the vine and you are the branches. Just as the branch cannot produce fruit unless it remains in the vine, so you cannot produce fruit unless you remain in me," and immediately adds, "Without me you are not able to do anything" [John 15:4–5]. Similarly, in another passage he says a bad tree cannot produce good fruit because the root has to be good before good fruit can be expected from it [Matt. 7:17–18]. We cannot be good trees, though, before we are grafted into Christ. That grafting is called *rebirth* in Scripture. Just as nobody contributes anything to his own *birth*, so nobody can contribute anything to his own *rebirth*. In this same[5] letter Paul also says that everything that does not proceed from faith is sin [Rom. 14:23]. Therefore, since the ungodly do not have faith, whatever they do must be considered sin. "If your eye is whole, your entire body will be illumined, but if your light is darkness, how great will the darkness be"

---

5. I.e., Romans.

[Matt. 6:22–23]! Unless faith is present, we dwell in darkness and necessarily remain stuck in our sins.

Furthermore, if we follow the Scholastics' opinion, we completely distort the nature of grace. If grace proceeds from works, Paul says, it ceases to be grace [Rom. 11:6]. He also adds that in seeking after the law of righteousness the Israelites did not attain to righteousness because they had sought it on the basis of works, not faith [Rom. 9:31–32]. To the Colossians as well he makes it perfectly clear what we are like before we are justified, "alienated from God, hostile in mind, in evil deeds" [1:21]. And in this letter to the Romans he calls individuals who have not yet been grafted into Christ wild olive trees, and we know that wild olive trees are barren and cannot produce fruit [11:24].

Furthermore, works cannot be good, unless they either satisfy the law or, wherever they fall short of the law, it is not imputed to them through Christ. But individuals who are not yet reborn are not able to satisfy the law, since not even the ones who *are* reborn can. Neither can they lay hold of the benefit of Christ, by which those who are broken are repaired, since they are not joined to him through faith. And the one who teaches that a person can do works that are pleasing to God without grace must also teach that Christ is not the redeemer of the whole person, since the one who teaches that we can do good and live rightly without Christ's grace is attributing no small portion of our salvation to our own nature. Paul also says in this passage, "When we were slaves to sin, we were free from righteousness" [Rom. 6:20]. This means nothing else but that we had absolutely no relationship or dealings with righteousness. Moreover, he exhorts us to serve righteousness just as we served sin, and he also wants us to serve righteousness now without any *sin* whatsoever; therefore, previously we served sin without any *righteousness* whatsoever. Finally, he has left no middle ground between slavery to sin and slavery to righteousness. Yet the Scholastics fabricate some suppositious individuals who though not yet justified still perform just and good acts that can find God's approval. All these considerations are sufficient to show how ridiculous and senseless their opinion is.

9. Meanwhile, they clamor that we are blasphemous to declare that man's entire nature is wicked. But, as Augustine wisely writes, "Behind the praises of nature hide the enemies of grace."[6] They should have considered to what source we refer this evil we decry. We do not attribute it to nature *as it was* created or to God, but to sin, which was given entrance through the first man. We differ in every way from the Manicheans, who fancied that nature was evil and created by an evil god.[7] We on the other hand confess and recognize that man was created free. As for his now having lost his freedom, we attribute that not to God as the author, but to man's own vice.

"Those who denied free will were called heretics by the Church."[8] This is to be understood as regarding the first creation of our nature. Otherwise there is not a single

---

6. The Latin reads *sub laudibus naturae latent inimici gratiae*. There is a tradition larger than Vermigli that attributes this pithy phrase to Augustine, yet the present writer has been unable to locate it in any of the extant writings of the bishop of Hippo.

7. See *On the Law*, section 2 for a direct rebuttal of Manichaeism.

8. Vermigli entertains a possible objection here to his position, a rhetorical figure known as *hypophora*.

Father who does not, if the truth is carefully examined, deplore man's wretched condition into which he has fallen through sin. Rather, it is our opponents who resemble the Manichees, who maintain that our corrupt affections were created in their current state by God and thus assert that evil was created by him.[9] We, on the other hand, recognizing that unruly affections are not free of sin, maintain that they were not created by God, and that instead it was our fault that they became unrestrained and hostile to the Word of God. It is true that in the beginning man was made in the image of God and that nothing is more fitting for him than freedom, but now that that image has been all but obliterated in us, so as to require restoration through Christ, is it any wonder that freedom as well has been largely lost? When they reason that man is free, it is like saying since man must be a two-footed creature, he is able to walk upright.[10] But if they drew this conclusion concerning a handicapped person, how wrong they would be, becomes unmistakably clear. The attributes of man that would be consonant with his unimpaired nature are incongruous when they are applied to his fallen nature.

---

9. A nice *peritropē* (περιτροπή), or turning the accusation of one's opponent back on himself, another rhetorical technique much practiced in classical and humanist rhetoric.

10. Romans 1558, Zürich 1580, Heidelberg 1603: *incedere* (so Marten). London 1576: *incidere*.

[CHAPTER 5:
THE CASE OF CORNELIUS]

Our opponents' conclusions are also not far from those of the Pelagians. The latter taught that our nature, aided by the grace of creation and the teachings of the law, is able to do good, while the former say that our nature, aided by a prevening and knocking[1] grace, is able to do good works that are pleasing to God. The orthodox Church opposed the Pelagians. It did not trouble itself with the grace of creation or that of the law or with a "prevening" grace, but taught that nobody is able to do good without the grace of Christ, by which we are justified. Moreover, for Augustine, who battled bravely against the Pelagians, there is no difference between doing good without grace and doing good outside of faith in Christ. In order to show that there is no good work without faith, he writes on Psalm 31, "Good intention renders a work good, and faith directs

---

1. The idea of knocking here derives from Revelation 3:20, which reads, "Behold, I stand at the door and knock. If anyone hears my voice and opens the door, I will come in to him and eat with him, and he with me" (ESV).

the intention." Therefore, do not look at what one does, but what he intends when he does it.[2]

10. Whereas in all of Scripture there is not a sentence that calls our doctrine into question, our opponents never cease citing to us in objection the case of Cornelius who, when still not yet reborn (as they suppose) and not yet believing in Christ, did works that were pleasing to God. We do indeed admit that Cornelius's almsgiving and prayers were pleasing to God, for the angel confirmed it, but the idea that he was not yet justified and did not yet believe in Christ when he did these things is their own invention. They do not take note that in this passage Scripture calls him godly (εὐσεβής) and God-fearing (φοβούμενος τὸν θεόν). So Cornelius was a believer, and in the Messiah at that, having been instructed by the teaching of the Jews; only, he did not know for sure if Jesus of Nazareth was that Messiah, and for that reason Peter is sent to teach him more fully.

But here, in order to pull the wool over our eyes, they say that, in chapter 17 of Acts, Paul attributes to the Athenians a degree of godliness, though in point of fact they were idol worshipers. He says, "Men of Athens, I proclaim to you the God whom unbeknownst to yourselves you revere (εὐσεβεῖτε)" [17:22–23]. Now, if one draws a letter of the alphabet well, he will not be called a scribe on that account. And whoever sings one or two songs is not therefore to be deemed a singer, because these designations call for knowledge and skill. Still, every now and then some-

2. Vermigli is most likely citing Augustine indirectly through Peter Lombard (*Sentences* 2. d. 40. c. 3), who does not refer to Augustine's exposition of Psalm 31, but rather to his *De mendacio* (*On Lying*).

body can by chance make a good drawing or sing a good song. In the same way, somebody who produces one or two works that have some appearance of godliness is not be considered, truly and unequivocally, godly.

What is more, Paul did not call the Athenians godly without adding two qualifications to extenuate their godliness. He says, "unbeknownst you revere" (ἀγνοοῦντες εὐσεβεῖτε). Yet what kind of godliness can be combined with ignorance of the true God? Moreover, shortly before, he called them δεισιδαιμονεστέρους, that is, rather superstitious [Acts 17:22]. Through these two words he minimizes their godliness a great deal. On the other hand, Luke calls Cornelius godly (εὐσεβής) without qualification and adds "God-fearing" (φοβούμενος τὸν θεόν). This addition is so important that in Job the man who fears God is translated in the Septuagint as genuine (ἀληθινός) and religious (θεοσεβής) [1:1]. Similarly, David says, "Blessed is the man who fears the LORD" [Psalm 112:1]. Now if he who fears God is blessed, how can he not also be justified?

Besides these points that prove the justification of Cornelius on the basis of *cause*, as it were, one can also add the testimony of *effect*. He gave alms that were pleasing to God. Now, we have by now, using many proofs, made it abundantly clear that nobody can do works that are pleasing to God except the one who is justified and reborn. Moreover, he distributed these alms to the Jews, so that giving something of his own earthly goods he might remunerate those who had instructed him in godliness, since it is fitting, as Paul teaches in Galatians, for the catechized to share all his goods with the catechizer [6:6]. Furthermore, the soldier sent to Peter clearly states that Cornelius had a good reputation among all the Jews. All this quite clearly shows that, even though we do not read that he was circumcised, he had so espoused the teaching of God's people as to be commended by all for his godliness. In addition to this, it is written that he prayed, and constantly at that. If we consider the entire story carefully, we will find that he observed the hour the Jews reserved for common prayers, since he says that he saw an angel standing by him at the ninth hour, who declared that his prayer had been heard. Yet in Isaiah 1, Proverbs 15, and several other places, we are told that the ungodly and sinners are not heard by God (this, however, is to be taken as meaning as long as they wish to be sinners and hold on to the will to sin).

11. What Augustine writes against the Donatists, that the prayers of immoral priests are heard by God, is not inconsistent with this interpretation, since he adds that this is the case because of the people's devotion. Cornelius, however, was aided by his own faith in his prayers, not that of bystanders. Augustine also says in his *Letter to Sixtus* that when justifying a person, God typically confers his Spirit on him so that he can make the petitions that will bring about salvation.[3] Since that is what Cornelius prayed, there can be no doubt that he was justified. Add to this the fact that nobody can properly entreat God except on the basis of faith, and it is by now quite manifest and established that we are justified by faith. Before he began to preach to Cornelius, Peter says that he indeed recognized that God was no respecter of persons, but that the one who does what is right is accepted before him, no

---

3. See Letter 194 (sections 16–17), in *The Works of Saint Augustine: A Translation for the 21ˢᵗ Century*, vol. II/3, trans. Roland Teske (Hyde Park, NY: New City, 1990), 295–96.

matter what nation he is in. These words clearly show that Cornelius was already accepted before God before Peter came to him.

I am surprised that there exist those who have the audacity to assert that he did not have faith in Christ, since in John 8 Christ himself says that the one who does not believe in the Son of God does not know God, and in John 4 he teaches his disciples, "If you believe in God, believe in me as well" [14:1], and, "if you believed Moses, you would also believe Me" [5:46]. These passages convince me that Cornelius truly believed in God and for that reason believed in the coming Messiah as well, just as he had been taught by the Jews, though he did not know that he had come and was Jesus of Nazareth, whom the Jews had driven to the cross. He had the faith by which the Patriarchs believed in a coming Christ. And so, since they were justified by that faith, how dare we deny Cornelius the very same thing?

Nathaniel, who believed in the coming Messiah, yet did not think that he had come yet, is proclaimed by Christ to be a true Israelite "in whom there is no guile" [John 1:47]. These two characteristics cannot come together in an individual who is not yet justified. Indeed, Peter was sent to Cornelius precisely so that he would know with greater clarity and perspicacity what he had believed about Christ obscurely. This was Gregory's view in *Homily 19 on Ezekiel*. He says faith is the antechamber, through which one arrives at good works, and not reversely: one does not arrive at faith from works. He concludes that Cornelius believed before he was able to perform praiseworthy deeds, and he cites the well-known passage in Hebrews,

"It is impossible to please God without faith" [11:6].[4] This statement can only be understood in the context of justifying faith, as is quite clear from the passage itself. In his commentary on Acts 10, Bede subscribes to the same interpretation and cites Gregory's words.[5] The teacher of the *Sentences* in book two, distinction twenty-five agrees as well.[6]

---

4. Pope Gregory (the Great), *Homiliae in Ezekielem Prophetam* 2.7.9 (*PL* 76:118).

5. J. A. Giles, *The Complete Works of Venerable Bede* (London: Whitaker and Co., 1844), 48.

6. Peter Lombard, *Sentences* 2.25.

[CHAPTER 6:
AUGUSTINE'S DYNAMIC VIEW OF
GRACE & FAITH AND ITS BEARING
ON THE CORNELIUS CASE]

But our opponents cite chapter seven of Augustine's *De Praedestinatione sanctorum* against us, where he argues against those who taught that faith is from us. While they granted that works were subsequent and from God, they maintained that they were obtained through faith. True, Augustine admits that works that follow faith are from God, but he denies that faith is from ourselves. Paul writes, he says, to the Ephesians, "You have been saved by grace through faith, and this is not from you: It is the gift of God" [Eph. 2:8–9]. But what he adds is a problem: "Cornelius's prayers and alms were accepted before God before he believed in Christ."

However, one must consider what follows. Augustine adds, "Yet he did not pray or give without a degree of faith. For how did he call upon one he did not believe in?" These words sufficiently show that Augustine does not deny Cornelius *all* faith in Christ, but only an explicit and limited faith. This is proven above all in the passage cited from Romans: "How will they call upon one in whom they have not believed?" [Rom. 10:14]. These words are written regarding the faith of regenerate individuals and their invocation, as the immediately preceding sentence clearly shows: "Every person who calls upon the name of the Lord will be saved" [Rom. 10:13], for we cannot attribute salvation to any but the justified. Peter was sent to Cornelius in order to build up, not to lay the foundation; the foundation of faith had already been laid in him.

12. But what Augustine goes on to say seems to occasion a greater difficulty. He says, "But if he were able to be saved without faith, that is, without faith in Christ, the Apostle would not have been sent as an architect for his building up." However, since he has already attributed to him faith and invocation, which salvation necessarily follows (and the Apostle writes about this in this letter),[1] how can he deny him salvation, unless we understand that in justified persons faith and salvation are not perfect while they live on this earth? In this life our salvation does not reach the point or the magnitude Christ requires in his elect. No one can doubt that before the resurrection and eternal salvation we are not going to have a perfect salvation, although we do enjoy it now in an inchoate state. Whereas in Ephesians Paul affirms that we have already been saved as a result of faith [Eph. 2:8], in Philippians he urges us to work out our own salvation with fear and trembling [Phil. 2:12].

These passages cannot be reconciled unless we say that salvation, having been begun in us through justifica-

---

1. I.e., Romans.

tion, is every day in the process of being perfected. We are always being restored more and more; our faith is being rendered fuller, more explicit, and more efficacious. If we do not take these words of Augustine in this way, either they are not his or he is contradicting himself. Now, we cannot deny that the book is Augustine's. Nor is it likely that he is contradicting himself. And if you say that these passages can agree with each other if we concede that Cornelius was not yet justified, though he did some works that were pleasing and accepted before God, I respond that that assertion cannot in any way be consonant with Augustine's opinion. For in his *Tractate on John* 81,[2] in *Against Julian* 4.3, and when commenting on Psalm 31, he uses compelling arguments and proves that all works that are done before we are justified are sins.[3]

That said, we can easily learn from what Christ said to the apostles that faith in those who are justified gets developed and perfected: "Many kings and prophets wanted to see the things you all see, yet did not see" [Luke 10:24]. Those kings and prophets were nonetheless godly and justified, although they had not understood all of Christ's mysteries as fully as the apostles. Similarly, in his prayer Christ declared concerning the apostles, "The words that you gave to me I have given to them; they have received them, and have recognized that I have come from you and

---

2. All the printed copies consulted read 801.

3. Augustine, *Tractatus super Ioannem* 81 (*Homilies on the Gospel of John*, NPNF 1/7:345–46); *Contra Iulianum* 4.3 (*The Fathers of the Church: Against Julian*, vol. 35, trans. Matthew Schumacher [New York: Fathers of the Church, 1957], 176–98); *Enarrationes in psalmos* 31 (*Expositions on the Psalms*, NPNF 1/8:70–71).

that you sent me" [John 17:8]. This shows that the apostles believed in Christ and were for that reason justified, although the actual Gospel narrative plainly indicates that there were many things they did not know. It is often related how they either had closed eyes, lest they see, or failed to understand what was being said. Therefore, Augustine does not completely deny salvation to Cornelius before Peter was sent to him; he only denies him a full-fledged and perfect one.

13. Likewise, they further cite in objection book two, question two of Augustine's *Quaestiones ad Simplicianum*, where he clearly teaches that faith precedes good works.[4] He then places something between grace and the celebration of the sacraments, saying that it is possible for a catechumen, and one who is still associated with catechumens, to believe and be recipients of grace, yet not yet be washed in baptism. What is more, he says that after the sacraments a fuller grace is poured in, by which he means that while the grace is the same, it is rendered more abundant. And so that you can rest assured that he is dealing with justifying faith he cites Ephesians, "You have been saved by grace through faith, and that not from yourselves; it is the gift of God" [Eph. 2:8].

Our opponents will say that they, too, teach that grace precedes good works and that from that grace a kind of faith is granted to people, but these bestowments are too weak in the beginning to be able to have the power to justify, yet certain works can be performed that are pleasing to God. However, let us remember what Augustine

---

4. Augustine, *Quaestiones ad Simplicianum* Book 2, Question 2 (*PL* 40:138–42).

writes about Pelagius in *Letter 105* to Innocent, Bishop of Rome.[5] He says that, at the Council of Palestine, Pelagius, to avoid being anathematized, anathematized all those who said that they were able to live rightly without grace. Yet by *grace* he understood nothing but the gifts bestowed upon us at creation, such as free will, reason, will, and the teaching of the law. Deceived by this trick, the Palestinian bishops absolved him.

Augustine excuses them on the grounds that they acted trustingly and guilelessly. When they heard Pelagius confess the grace of God, they could not fathom another one besides the ones that Scripture proclaimed; namely, the one through which we are regenerated and grafted into Christ. It is therefore clear that those who fabricate a grace for themselves other than the one by which we are justified and grafted into Christ foist a human invention upon us, or rather a Pelagian subterfuge that Scripture does not recognize. Secondly, in the passage we just now mentioned, Augustine states that although catechumens and believers have not been baptized, they have still been *conceived*. Now, those who have already been conceived so as to be children of God cannot be strangers or enemies to him. It therefore follows that they have already been justified, just not completely. This is apparent from the fact that Augustine calls the grace that follows *fuller*, since it differs from the preceding one not in kind or nature, but only in degree and magnitude. Since this grace belongs to the same species as the other, it will justify as well.

---

5. This statement is in fact made in Letter 194, section 7 (addressed to Sixtus), found in *Works of Saint Augustine*, vol. II/3, 292.

This is quite clear from the fact that Cornelius is said to have done works that pleased God. It is not very significant that Augustine adds that that grace was not sufficiently great for either Cornelius or catechumens to gain the kingdom of Heaven.[6] These words do not establish the rule that after this grace, or the faith of the catechumens, another one, which justifies, is forthcoming, as though they had not been justified by the previous one. He only meant to show that catechumens should not stop at that point in faith and grace, but should receive baptism and move forward until their salvation and regeneration, which had been begun, was made complete. For if one held the sacrament of baptism in light esteem, he would be shut off from the kingdom of Heaven, since those who have believed ought to be concerned first and foremost with being grafted into the Church through the sacrament. Those who either refuse or neglect doing so show clearly enough that they have not sincerely believed.

Therefore, it is not absurd to say that Cornelius (and the catechumens) had a grace that did justify, but would not have sufficed for reaching the kingdom of Heaven if he had disregarded baptism. That Augustine had this in mind is shown by what he adds; namely, that one must not only be conceived, but born as well. This should be understood as meaning *unless a legitimate obstacle stands in the way*. Augustine will not deny salvation to one who believes and desires baptism, yet is unable to obtain it. Together with the other Fathers he acknowledges that

6. Cf. Augustine, *De baptismo contra Donatistas* 21–29 (*On Baptism, Against the Donatists, NPNF* 1/4:459–60).

there is an inward baptism[7] and that the power of the Holy Spirit works in our souls without external symbols. This is shown in question 84 of his *On Leviticus*, which says Moses had a sacerdotal grace without an external ordination to the priesthood and without visible signs, that John the Baptist was imbued with the Holy Spirit in his mother's womb without external sacraments, and that the thief on the cross was saved by God's grace alone without any sacraments.[8]

Finally, from his saying that we are conceived by that prior grace of God and born by the subsequent one it is quite clear that the one who is conceived and the one who is born belong to the same species, since a living organism does not have a different nature when it is conceived than when it is brought forth. The only difference is that the one is more complete, the other less so. Accordingly, when he is baptized, a catechumen can be considered more complete thanks to the grace he receives in baptism than he was before when he only believed, although at that time as well he was justified through faith, by which he embraced the promises of God in Christ.

---

7. Vermigli calls this *baptismus flaminis*, defined as "the special gifts of the Spirit poured out on the church," in Richard Muller, *Dictionary of Latin and Greek Theological Terms*, 2nd ed. (Grand Rapids: Baker Academic Press, 2017), s.l. "baptismus flaminis."

8. Augustine, *On Leviticus*, question 84 (*PL* 34:712).

[CHAPTER 7:
CHRYSOSTOM ON THE
CASE OF CORNELIUS]

14. It remains for us now to examine a passage of Chrysostom's in his *Homilia de spiritu, natura et lege*.[1] If required to be frank, though, the speech does not seem to me to be his, since it is inconsistent with itself and contains unresolvable propositions that cannot in any way be reconciled. But, whoever it is, it supports us more so than our opponents. He says first that compassionate individuals enjoy no fruit from their almsgiving until they have faith. As soon as one *is* adorned with faith, good and fruit-bearing works immediately follow; but before that, they are nonexistent. He also adds that we are saved by faith alone, since works without faith were never able to

---

1. Vermigli is referring to what now goes by the title *De fide et lege naturae et Sancto Spiritu sermo* (*Sermon on Faith, Natural Law, and the Holy Spirit*), found in *PG* 48:1081–88, and included there in the spurious works attributed to Chrysostom.

save those who performed them. He cites the thief who he affirms was saved by faith alone without works.[2]

And so as to leave no doubt as to what faith he is discussing, he is discussing that faith by which we are made citizens of Heaven and friends of God, characteristics that can only be ascribed to justifying faith. Moreover, categorically stating that there is no good outside faith, he offers in support of his assertion the fact that the soul that does not have faith is dead, and to make his point clearer he says that those who perform outstanding works without faith are like corpses and the remains of the dead. Though they are adorned with garments that are lovely and costly, still they have no awareness of them, derive no warmth from them, and are not protected by them from corruption. Thus he says that although they sometimes seem to do good, even so they derive no benefit from their works. He then goes on to say that just as it is necessary for a person to be alive first before food can be given to him so that he can be nourished, so it is necessary for faith first to exist, and then be nourished by good works. Concerning Cornelius's deeds he says that they were admirable and pleasing to God, the Incomparable Remunerator. All these ideas are stated truthfully and in accord with our teaching.

Later, though, he adds that Cornelius had not yet believed in Christ when he did the works that are praised. While this is a hard saying, it can be rendered less so by interpretation, if we understand him as not yet having believed distinctly and explicitly, as we argued in the case of Augustine. Nevertheless, that he had believed in Christ in the same way as the saints of old whose salvation through

---

2. *Sermon on Faith, Natural Law, and the Holy Spirit* (*PL* 48:1082).

the Savior they were awaiting we do not doubt. This kind of faith was enough for their salvation until such time as the Gospel should be made known. He subsequently adds that Cornelius could not have obtained salvation if he had not received faith, but this could still be granted if the statement is taken to refer to the perfected salvation that Christians are called to and shall one day be brought to.

However, what he goes on to write cannot[3] in any way be consistent. He says that Cornelius's works were dead. It is at this point that Chrysostom begins not being Chrysostom. How could Cornelius's works have been admirable and pleasing to God the Incomparable Remunerator, if they were dead? On the other hand, if we wish to ascertain the real opinion of Chrysostom himself on this question, let us consider what he writes on this story in Acts 9. There he unmistakably declares that Cornelius believed and was a godly man. Not content with this, he adds that his life was upright and he held sound beliefs. In so speaking he affirms that he both had faith and the fruit of faith as well. Finally, he adds that he had faith, righteousness, and all virtue. So much therefore concerning Chrysostom.

---

3. Romans 1558, Zürich 1580, Heidelberg 1603: *potest*. London 1576: *om.*

[CHAPTER 8:
VIRTUOUS DEEDS OUTSIDE
OF CHRIST ARE SINS]

Yet their rejoinder to this position of ours is that the out-standing deeds of the Romans and their remarkable accomplishments were remunerated by God with the reward of a vast empire. To support this idea they cite Augustine's *City of God* 5.15 where he says that God bestowed on those to whom he was not going to give eternal life the terrestrial glory of a surpassing empire.[1] If he had not done so, there would be no reward given to their good practices, that is, their virtues, by which they strove to reach such a pinnacle of glory.

15. In order, however, to understand this remuneration that Augustine discusses we should reflect on the fact that in his governance of the world God wishes everything to be carried out in a certain order and without confusion, so that effects will follow their causes and characteristics will be attached to the things they belong to. Crops ripen

---

1. Augustine, *De civitate Dei* 2.15 (*City of God*, NPNF 1/2:97).

at the sun's heat. Good pursuits follow upon an intelligent man's hard work and application. Spring replaces winter, summer in turn replaces springtime, and fall summer. Plants produce leaves, then flowers, then fruit. In this way God makes provision for nature, communities, and families, and because human civilization would fall apart if governments characterized by laws and virtues were not in control, it stands to reason, by order of God and the arrangement of nature, that wherever military discipline, obedience towards magistrates, maintenance of the laws, rigorous exercise of justice, honorable conduct of princes, self-restraint, bravery, and love of one's country flourish, there a great dominion is a matter of course.

This does not mean, though, that those[2] actions are not sins, since they proceed from human beings without faith and do not aim at the glory of God, which ought to be the goal of all human actions. Accordingly, whenever this glory and vastness of dominion results from moral and civil virtues according to the ordinance of God and is regarded by statesmen as their end-goal,[3] it is called the fruit of their labors and their reward. However, Augustine himself in chapter twelve of the same book of *City of God* asserts that those deeds of the Romans were sins "because," as he writes of the Romans, "for the sake of honor, praise, and glory they attended to their country's welfare, in which they sought glory itself and did not hesitate to

---

2. London 1576: *ulla* (any). Romans 1558, Zürich 1580, and Heidelberg 1603: *illa* (those).

3. London 1576: *fines et fructus*. Romans 1558, Zürich 1580: *finis et fructus*. Heidelberg 1603: *finis fructus*. The later Heidelberg edition appears to have the better reading.

put its welfare in front of their own, squashing the love of money and many other vices on behalf of this one vice, namely, love of praise."[4] Here he calls the ambition of the Romans a vice. Who therefore would say that God in a real or actual sense rewards sins?

What is left, therefore, is for this remuneration to be understood as we have argued; namely, as something that results from the natural arrangement established by God and is held by those on whom it is bestowed to be the reward and fruit of their labors. For even Scripture has used this expression in several places: concerning the scribes and hypocrites the Lord says, "Truly I say to you, they have received their reward" [Matt. 6:2]. Regarding those who, though they knew God, did not worship him as God, Paul says, "But given over to shameful desires they treated their bodies with disgrace[5] and violence" [Rom. 1:24] and "They received in themselves their fitting reward" [Rom. 1:27]. In chapter 29 Ezekiel says that God wishes to reward Nebuchadnezzar for serving him in the levelling of Tyre and by way of reward promises him the destruction and plundering of Egypt [vv. 19–20]. However, the works of the hypocrites who disfigured their faces in order to appear to people to be fasting, and the superstitious and execrable ceremonies of the idol worshipers, as well as the cruel deeds Nebuchadnezzar performed in order to glut his own ambition, were beyond all doubt sins, and serious ones at that. Yet we read that they all

---

4. Augustine, *De civitate Dei* 5.12 (*City of God*, NPNF 1/2:94).

5. London 1576: *ignominiae*. Romans 1558, Zürich 1580, and Heidelberg 1603: *ignominia*.

received a reward. But Augustine himself clearly instructs us in *City of God* 2.12 (a passage we have already cited) that in establishing the other empires God had something different in mind than disbursing a reward to these individuals: whereas previously the foremost rule had been in the East, God at length willed that Roman rule should hold sway in order for it to suppress the misdeeds of all the other nations.[6]

16. But many suspect that as a result of this teaching a window is opened to many vices, since if all the actions of individuals, who in a civil context appear to behave virtuously, are all sins, they will easily be deterred from honorable deeds. My response is that I am not advocating a slackening of civil discipline, which according to God's providence is a kind of fetter, as it were, by which civil harmony is preserved. God can indeed abide communities and governments for as long as moral integrity and virtue thrive in them, but when one becomes thoroughly depraved and corrupt, God is provoked to anger and desires to exact the punishment from it that up until then he had for a long time ignored. Men *do* sin as long as they are outside of Christ, even when they perform excellent deeds, but they do so much less than if they threw off all civil responsibilities and completely devoted themselves to all of the vices. We are not Stoics, and so do not think that all sins are equal. Moreover, if such individuals give up doing the things which by the very light of their reason they recognize to be virtuous, they come into opposition with their conscience.

---

6. Augustine, *De civitate Dei* 2.15 (*City of God*, NPNF 1/2:93–96).

And if we wish to see more clearly which position, ours or our opponents', opens up a bigger window to vices, let us compare the one with the other. Obviously, when they maintain that the ungodly are able to do good works that are pleasing to God, and are able by them to merit grace "congruently" (to use their language),[7] what else do they do but give false hope and encouragement to wretched souls in the doomed state they are in? For they cause them to be complacent on account of some good works or other of their own and to expect that because of them they will, at the end of their life at least, gain from God a true and sincere conversion. Meanwhile, though, living without a care in the world, they do not renounce their misdeeds in authentic and true repentance. When we, on the other hand, daily admonish them to come to Christ and be reconciled through true repentance, since otherwise their good works are not going to benefit them in the slightest, seeing that however resplendent they may be they are still sins in God's sight, do we not powerfully spur them on to abandon their ungodliness and corrupt manner of life and turn themselves to God's righteousness? If you weigh these considerations wisely, you will easily perceive which of us opens up more of a way to sinful desires.

Everyone who is moved by any fondness for truth and godliness will certainly judge so. Apart from what I have said, they will easily recognize that everything good that is attributed to unregenerate men is subtracted and taken away from God's grace, since if apart from God's grace we can perform many things that are gratifying and pleasing to him, it follows that we have not been entirely

---

7. The technical term Vermigli is referring to is *de congruo*.

51

redeemed and restored by him, an idea so impious and at odds with the catholic truth that nothing more shameful or impious can be conceived! What godliness is there left, when Christ is robbed of his honor? Or what honor is left to Christ if we teach that he did not confer on us all our ability to live uprightly?

[CHAPTER 9:
THE VALUE OF DEEDS
INSTRUMENTAL TO SALVATION]

A few people submit that many things at times take place and are done before regeneration that are a kind of means, so to speak, towards obtaining regeneration, and since it often happens that we are justified through them they cannot be considered sins. We do certainly acknowledge that there are at times such means, through which God brings us to justification, but one cannot conclude from this that they are not sins to those by whom they are done. At any rate, as far as the nature of the works themselves is concerned, to some people they are occasions for greater destruction. For you could find several people who on account of such works of theirs pride themselves with astonishing self-satisfaction, place themselves before others and, full and bloated from a high opinion of themselves, refuse to progress further, though urged on and encouraged. In the case of these persons such works are a preparation for eternal death. In contrast, as far as the elect are concerned, God controls and guides their works and sees to it that they contribute to their salvation, although by their nature they are sins and must be considered sinful as long as the light of justification has not shone upon them. We therefore admit that works are a kind of preparation towards a turning to salvation, but only for the predestined and elect whom God leads to justification at times through these works—not that they themselves *by their own nature* have the power of making preparations for justification, since for the rejected and reprobate they work towards their condemnation.

17. Yet let us see just what those things are that our opponents praise so much in the case of unregenerate persons. "There is," they say, "a certain recognition of sin in them, out of which a fright is born that hounds them. Subsequently, there is stirred up a grief over losing the kingdom of Heaven, and they gravitate to wicked deeds with less fondness and derive less pleasure from the sins and temptations of this world. They even appear to hear the Word of God with a degree of interest. These things," they say, "how can they be considered sins, even though they are not effectual enough for a man to be converted through them and abandon his former state of depravity?"

Here I will seek some information from these individuals: what exactly is that awareness of sin which we possess, yet still prefer sin to God's righteousness? Since it lacks its proper and peculiar end, it clearly cannot but be sin. For the basic point of that awareness is that we should leave our sin once we become cognizant of it and embrace God's righteousness. If this end is not present, the work is ruined and becomes sin. All the pagan writers acknowledge that an action whose proper end is taken away is a sin.

Secondly, what is that fear of Hell, when they continue daily to hurl themselves into it? And what is that grief over losing the kingdom of Heaven, when they constantly decline it when Scripture and preachers offer it to them? Though they gravitate with less fondness towards sinning and derive less pleasure from their sins, they still derive enough that they cannot be torn away from them. Though they hear the Word of God with a degree of interest, they nevertheless show contempt for the hearing, since they expect they will gain the things that are promised in it, even though they live as they do. We see therefore that all these promptings veer from their target and destined end. And since they all are far from effectual and leave men under God's anger, nothing good can be expected from them. But let us hear what Isaiah relates in chapter 58 concerning this class of works. He says:

> Throughout each day they seek me and wish to know my ways, like a nation that has done justice and has not disregarded the judgment of its God. They consult me concerning just judgments and wish to draw near to God. "Why did we fast and you did not see," they say. "Why have we afflicted our souls and you do not acknowledge it?" Behold, the day on which you fast you find what you desire, and you all demand your debts. Behold, you fast for lawsuits and actions, so that you may strike with a fist. Surely such is not the fasting that I have chosen [vv. 2–5].

These words of the prophet show quite clearly that it is sin in the sight of God to consult him concerning his ways, to fast and wear oneself down with afflictions, when such works are rendered without true reverence for God and true godliness. It cannot be denied but that these works are indeed excellent and lovely, but God the Just Judge rejects them. In his *Confessions*, Augustine offers himself as a trustworthy example for us in this matter. He describes the feelings he experienced in his heart before turning to Christ. In book eight, chapter eleven he writes:

> I thrashed about in my bondage until it should be broken off completely. In it I was held and, though it was by now narrow, I was held nonetheless. You, Lord, redoubled in my sight[1] the lashes of fear and shame with a stern mercy. Inwardly I said within myself, "Come, let it happen now." Now I almost resolved, yet did not do it. A little less [was needed], and I was on the verge of touching and holding it, yet did not touch and did not hold it. Stronger in me was the ingrained worse impulse than the better unfamiliar one. The closer the point of time approached at which I was going to be something else, the vaster the fright it struck me with. Trifles of trifles and vanities of vanities held me

1. Romans 1558, London 1576, Zürich 1580, and Heidelberg 1603 all read *in oculis meis*. Modern editions of the *Confessions* read *in occultis meis*, "in my inward parts." It appears that the manuscripts Vermigli had were different both in this and in other respects, as this entire passage as quoted by Vermigli leaves out much from the original passage in *Confessions*, unless it is due to Vermigli's quoting from memory.

back, my old dalliances, who whispered, "Are you tossing us aside? And from that moment will we not be with you forever? And from that moment will this and that no longer be permitted to you forever?" I heard them now much less than half-way.[2]

These are the things he relates, and he denounces them before God as sins, yet these opponents of ours praise them so very much. They were certainly means by which Augustine was brought by God to salvation, yet all the while they were sins in him. While he did not give himself over to them, he did corrupt them with many abuses so that he would not be changed by them. What is not fully realized as it ought to be is sin.

18. But the sophists are like hydras in a way. Once one argument has been lopped off like a head, another one sprouts up. They cite against us the publican who prayed in the temple: "God be favorable to me a sinner," and he is said to have returned home justified. "Therefore," they say, "he was a sinner when he prayed, since we read that he was later justified. Yet his prayer was pleasing to God. Therefore," they say, "we are able to do works pleasing to God *before* we are reborn." However, they should have kept in mind that the publican *prayed*—a thing which, just as we showed in the case of Cornelius, could not be done without faith. "For how will they call upon him in whom they have not believed" [Rom. 10:14]? He was justified therefore when he prayed, nor should you understand those

---

2. Augustine, *Confessiones* 8.11.25–26 [actually a conflation of sections 25 and 26] (*Confessions, NPNF* 1/1:126–27).

words to mean he was justified for the first time at the moment when he brought his prayers to an end. Even though it is said it happened afterwards, that does not mean that it had not happened in any way beforehand. He obtained a more complete justification, a fuller spirit, and a more intimate sense of divine mercy.

He calls himself a sinner, and rightly so, partly because he still felt in himself something he should find fault with (we are always told, however righteous we may be, to pray, "Forgive us our debts"), and partly because he remembered how serious the sins were that he committed before he was justified. And the saints ought to consider, especially during prayer, how great the burden of their sins is. For when in prayer they approach God, they are moved by true repentance to say with David, "My bones have wasted away in my moaning. Every day, by night and day, your hand is heavy upon me. My vigor is drained, as the moisture of the earth dries up in summer" [Psalm 32:3–4]. "My sins surrounded me without number. My iniquities surrounded me, so that I was not able to see. They have grown more numerous than the hairs of my head" [Psalm 40:12]. "My heart has deserted me. I recognize my misdeeds, and my sin is always in front of me. Against you, you I have sinned, and before you I have done evil" [Psalm 51:3–4]. And so that the saints will henceforth be all the more on their guard against sins, God stirs up in them a most poignant sense of his anger, so that they will realize what they deserved, if God had not come to their aid through his Son. He also opens up their eyes so that they will see what his fatherly correction towards them is; and so that this will be more clearly perceived, he often withholds from them the sense and taste of his mercy. For that reason they cry, "Cause me to hear joy and happiness, that my humbled bones may rejoice. Hide your face from my sins and erase all my iniquities. Create a pure heart in me, God, and renew deep inside me an upright spirit. Do not cast me away from your face, do not take away from me your Holy Spirit" [Psalm 51:8–11].

Hence even the justified pray that what weakness still remains not be imputed to them. They recall the grave sins they committed earlier and beseech but a taste of divine mercy and of the righteousness he conferred on them. This is the true meaning of such pious prayers, and we must not believe that the publican prayed any differently. His attitude was not one that meant to hold on to his erstwhile objective to sin; on the contrary, he was truly and sincerely turning to God. Our opponents, on the other hand, imagine that those who still persist in misdeeds and have not resolved to change their life still do something good that is pleasing to God. Yet we are taught by Scripture that the one who believes in God has eternal life and is for that reason justified; everything else is neither good nor pleasing to God. This being the case, since the publican prayed, and prayed faithfully, it is clear that he had eternal life and had a degree of justification as well.

[CHAPTER 10:
CHARACTERISTICS
OF A GOOD WORK]

19. But so that all this can be more clearly understood, it will not be out of place to review what the requirements are for a good work that is able to be gratifying to God. Firstly, the one who does something good must be animated by God's Spirit; if not, there dwells in us, that is, in our flesh, nothing good. And those who are driven by the Spirit of God are sons of God. Secondly, faith must be present so that through it we can know for certain that the work we are undertaking belongs to that class of things that God wants and has ordered to be done in his law. For "Everything that is not from faith is sin" [Rom. 14:23], nor should we commit the error of doing something our hearts find fault with us for. Thirdly, whatever we do must absolutely be directed to the glory of God, so that our chief and primary concern will be that the praise and glory of God be made apparent by our works: "Whether you eat or drink or do anything else, do it all to the glory of God" [1 Cor. 10:31], says Paul. Fourthly,

since, due to our innate feebleness, something is always
lacking in our works, even in those which seem to be done
correctly, God's grace and mercy must be present through
Christ, so that it can make up for that deficiency. For
this reason David says, "Blessed are those whose iniquities are forgiven. Blessed is the man to whom the LORD
has not imputed his sin" [Psalm 32:1–2]. And Paul says,
"There is therefore no condemnation against those who
are in Christ Jesus" [Rom. 8:1], and "What was impossible for the law, inasmuch as it was weakened through the
flesh, God, sending his Son, etc." [Rom. 8:3]. These passages show clearly that our works fall short of perfection
and their proper end and that through Christ and God's
mercy it is brought about that the blame that attaches
to them is not imputed to us. Lastly, it is also required
that nobody boast about what he does rightly, but that
he boast in God alone, and recognize that what he does
he has received from his generosity, not his own strength.
"For who," Paul says to the Corinthians, "has made you
different? What do you have that you did not receive?
And if you received it, why do you boast as though you
did not receive it?" [1 Cor. 4:7].

Where all these things that I have gone over are present, the work will be incontrovertibly good and pleasing
to God. Here the attentive reader can infer from these
requirements for a good work its definition. Conversely,
if we take a look at the nature of an individual not yet
regenerated, we will easily recognize that the things we
have established as necessary for a good work cannot be
found there. For that individual is entirely bereft of God's
Spirit and faith, and moreover suffers from such φιλαυτία,

that is, self-love,[1] that whatever he does he directs it not to God, but to his own advantage. What is more, since he is alien to Christ, he is necessarily left under the law, and so whatever deficiency or defect there is in his works (which is necessarily extensive), cannot be made up from anywhere else. Finally, if by chance he does do something splendid or lovely, he boasts not in God, but in himself, since he is ignorant of Christ and God's grace. From these two descriptions of a good and God-pleasing work and of a person living outside of Christ I think it is by now clear that those works that proceed from a person without faith cannot be good and pleasing to God.

20. But our opponents do their best to misconstrue two very compelling passages that we use for this discussion. The former is our saying that "a bad tree cannot produce good fruit" [Matt. 7:18]; the second, that "everything that is not from faith is sin" [Rom. 14:23]. We have to say something here about these passages. Christ used the metaphor of the bad tree that cannot produce good fruit not only in Matthew 7, but again in Matthew 12, and deduced from it the statement, "Brood of vipers, how can your speech be good, when you are wicked?" [Matt. 12:34]. However, before I unpack this harsh reproach, it will be worthwhile to relate how Augustine sparred with Julian the Pelagian in defense of this same passage.[2] He en-

---

1. This Greek word, φιλαυτία, occurs throughout Greek philosophy and is especially common in Stoic writers. Vermigli may very well use the Greek word here to imply that even the pagan philosophers concurred that such self-love was a prominent feature of human psychology.

2. Augustine, *Contra Iulianum* 4.3 (*Fathers of the Church*, 35:176–98).

tertains an excellent deed done by a person without faith, namely, clothing the naked, and asks whether it should be called a sin. And in point of fact, if this deed does not belong to the class that pleases God, I do not see what other deed which unbelievers do is able to be gratifying to him. Now, Augustine maintains, and proves, that it is sin. And lest he be thought to assert this without reason, he says it is sin because the one who did that so very beautiful deed boasts in the deed. He does not through faith recognize either God or Christ as the one to give the credit to.[3] He then says that, in order for there not to be sin, it is not enough for a good thing to be done; it must also be done well and rightly. Will we therefore say that a person without faith did a good work, and also performed it rightly? If we do not grant this, we acknowledge that he sinned; if we do grant it, we acknowledge that the fruit is good, though the person without faith and outside of Christ is a bad tree. In so doing, we grant that a bad tree produces good fruit, a thing that Christ, however, expressly denies.

Hence our opponents are reduced to the necessity of now openly disagreeing not only with us, but with Christ as well, unless of course they wish to say that a person without faith and alien to God is a good tree. Yet if this is what they claim, what do they mean when they say that he is not pleasing to God, since what is good cannot but be gratifying to a good God? But as it is, to be pleasing to God, one must by all means have faith, for it is written in Hebrews, "Without faith it is impossible to be pleasing

---

3. Romans 1558, London 1576: *cui id illud acceptum ferat*; Zürich 1580 and Heidelberg 1603: *cui is illud acceptum ferat*. The latter reading is the preferable one.

to God" [Heb. 11:6]. Yet these mean to thrust upon us through this heresy of theirs an idea that this epistle says is impossible.

"But a man," they say, "*qua* man, is not a bad tree." However, as Augustine says, if we take into account natures only, there will not be any bad tree anywhere, for both angels and men were created by God and received good natures. We must not regard these natures as they were created by God, but in light of the condition that later befell them. A person will be called a good tree, when endowed with a good will; a person will be called a bad tree, when endowed with a bad will. After the Fall of Adam and the original ruin of our race we speak of men as driven not by a good will, but a bad one.

But to return to the charitable act of the person without faith, which we began to discuss, we must ask whether this mercy that is shown is one of faith or one without it. Since it is performed without faith, it must be without it. Therefore, it cannot be free of vice and sin. It is not enough to have pity on one's neighbor; it must also be done in faith and rightly. Mercy is not good in and of itself, for God disapproved of many acts of kindness conferred on neighbors, as when the king of Israel spared the king of Syria and when Saul spared Agag, the king of Amalek. On the other hand, faith that works through love is always good and can never be bad. But since mercy is not of this sort, rightness must be added so that by it mercy can be performed in faith, so that it can be praiseworthy. They retort that this natural affection of having mercy is good. We are perhaps not inclined to deny this, but they ought to have realized that persons not yet regenerated abuse this good thing when they do not refer it to God, who is the sole end of all our actions; and of course one who perversely abuses so great a gift from God does not sin lightly.

21. Moreover, Augustine also asserts that whatever good there is in the work of a person without faith comes entirely from God. Therefore, the fact that one's neighbor is helped, some reasonable way of life is maintained, and civil virtue is preserved comes from nowhere else but God, though it is a sin and displeasing to God, insofar as it proceeds from a person corrupt and without faith. Pelagius was led by these and similar reasons to affirm that these individuals who thus by nature behave rightly are, to be sure, good, but fruitlessly so. Again, Augustine demurs, saying that such is the nature of fruitless trees that they either produce nothing at all or what is evil. Pelagius continues trying to make himself understood and says that they are to be called fruitless because, though what they do is good, they still are useless in obtaining the kingdom of Heaven. However, in saying this he says nothing; as a matter of fact, he produces more obstacles for himself.

As is clear, this is the same position of our Scholastics today, though Augustine battles it to the best of his ability, saying, "In that case, as you say, the Lord, being good, will uproot and cast into the fire a good plant that produces good fruit. What becomes of divine justice, which you all defend so strictly everywhere? This position of yours leads to many preposterous and absurd conclusions."[4] So much for Augustine. Our opponents, though,

---

4. Here Vermigli is not quoting Augustine, but, as was often done by the classical orators, speaks as though from his perspective, a type of

assert that they are much different than Pelagius. "We posit," they say, "a certain prevening and knocking⁵ grace by means of which a good treasure can be inserted in people's hearts so that they can thereby perform something good. Therefore, they will not be plants altogether dead, for in one way or another they put forth buds, and although what they produce cannot ripen into flowers and actual fruit, they are nonetheless foliage and leaves that can and do shoot forth from a modicum of the juice of God's grace which even those that are alien to Christ are not altogether destitute of."

However, Pelagius asserted this too, for he did not avoid the word grace, though he did, as Augustine cleverly reveals, understand by it what he wanted rather than what he ought, and much differently than what the word means in the catholic writers of Christ's Church or in Scripture. But they become too carried away in their metaphor. They fail to remember that the Lord in the Gospel cursed the tree that only had leaves without fruit and commanded it to be uprooted and thrown into the fire. Now, nothing but sin is subject to the curse⁶ of God and eternal fire.

---

personification (*prosopopoeia*). Similarly, the direct speech he places in the mouth of his Scholastic opponents is not meant to be taken literally, but an instance of *hypophora* (anticipating your opponent's argument), much practiced in classical and humanistic rhetoric.

5. See Chapter 5, footnote 1, above.

6. Romans 1558, London 1576, and Zürich 1580: *execratione*. Heidelberg 1603: *execrationi*. Once again the later Heidelberg has the better reading.

But they still have another tactic by which to evade this passage.[7] They say that those trees are indeed bad, but not completely dead, since *some* juice of grace is found in them. They argue that there is a certain knocking and prevening grace by which a good treasure can be inserted in the hearts of people who are not reborn, from which a tiny bud can be drawn out from an unrepentant person. Although they are not able to bring what they produce to the level of complete and ripe fruit or even bring forth flowers, they still put forth foliage and leaves—the bare minimum—and all this is certainly the sign of some latent grace and life.

It is incredible how much they plume themselves on this prevening and knocking grace, though we have already shown above what one should think of it.[8] Those who speak and think in these terms are too careless. They fail to perceive that this grace of theirs is nothing but a kind of invitation to come to Christ, though an ineffectual one, since people who have it are left under God's anger and their hearts are not changed. And so, what good treasure can there be in them which could produce works pleasing to God? What is more, to continue their metaphor, when they say that they are plants that produce foliage and leaves, even though they have no fruit, they should have recalled that Christ, as we said before, cursed such trees and when he sought fruit in the fig tree and

<hr/>

7. London 1576: *loco.* Romans 1558, Zürich 1580, and Heidelberg 1603: *locum.* The latter is the better reading.

8. See section 9 above.

found only leaves, leveled so powerful a curse at it that it withered up.

We do not deny that men can perform a civil and moral good which is produced through the power of God by which everything is maintained, for even the pagans acknowledged that "In him we live, move and have our being" [Acts 17:28].[9] But that power by which God rules and directs all things does not render persons who are not reborn a whit more fit for eternal life. But the stasis of our case at issue is whether those who are still alien to Christ can do something good that is approved and agreeable to God. This we deny, while they affirm it. How much the passage adduced regarding the bad tree that cannot produce good fruit is in our favor has been sufficiently indicated.

22. Now let us examine the second passage that they try to wrest from us: "Everything that is not from faith is sin" [Rom. 14:23]. Augustine brought up this passage on nearly every occasion against Pelagius, who would respond that this statement was particular only and spoken exclusively in the context of foods and for that reason ought not to be extended to cover other works, especially those of persons without faith. True, we acknowledge that this issue arose over foods, but let us examine with a view to the words of Paul himself how this statement is made. He says that the one who wavers, that is, the one who has doubts in either direction, yet eats, is condemned. This was what he had to prove. The reason he subsequently

---

9. Here Paul is quoting a line once attributed to Epimenides, but now thought to be of unknown, though ancient, origin, and labeled "pseudo-Epimenidean."

gave was: "Because it is not from faith." But, since this statement is merely particular and what is said cannot be reduced to a syllogism unless a major premise is added, Paul added, "Everything that is not from faith is sin." By this statement Paul wanted us to be certain that whatever we undertake doing is going to be pleasing to God and is required by him through one of the ordinances in the law. If this confidence is absent, whatever we do, he says, is sin. Paul's train of thought can be put together as follows: everything that is not from faith is sin; eating foods forbidden in the law with uncertainty as to whether it is permitted or not is not from faith; therefore, it is sin. Although the Apostle is proving the minor premise, he bases it on a universally applicable principle. This principle can be applied to all actions, just as it is applied to foods: *everything* that lacks faith is sin. Consequently, neither Augustine nor we ourselves do violence to this statement when we apply it to the works of unbelievers.

However, many today clamor and say that in this passage faith means the conviction of the conscience, and that Paul did not have in mind the faith that we say justifies. These people grant themselves too much liberty in introducing a new meaning to faith without any scriptural evidence. And so, we could refuse to grant them this. But since they are still compelled to admit the truth of our position even if we grant them what they want, we will not take them to task on this score. Let it be as they want, let faith be *conscience*. What should be the conviction of a conscience regarding works, so as to understand what works are good and what bad? Clearly we can have no other rule, if we are godly, than God's law. That is the measure by which good and bad must be judged. That is where our conscience must find conviction, because it is through faith that it understands the work it is undertaking is good and, by contrast, bad, if it is inconsistent with God's law. And this is the very thing we just said about faith. So, let us disregard those who say this. Though they claim to be saying something different from us, they end up unintentionally agreeing with us! We are taught here that in whatever action we undertake, we are first and foremost to make sure that we are certain about God's will, and Paul is the one who has taught this, when he says, "Let us prove (δοκιμάζωμεν) what God's good will is" [Rom. 12:2]. He also writes to the Ephesians, "Let us not walk as the unwise, not understanding what God's will is" [5:15–17].

And, reader, lest you think that this interpretation is a fabrication of our own, consult Origen,[10] Augustine's student Primasius,[11] and the commentary that is attributed to Jerome.[12] You will find that they say the same thing

---

10. Origen of Alexandria (ca. 183–253) was one of the most influential early Church Fathers and produced an enormous output of writings, only a fraction of which survives today.

11. The precise date of the birth of Primasius of Hadrumetum is unknown. He is thought to have died around AD 560. He was bishop of Hadrumetum and primate of Byzacena. He is known chiefly for his commentary on Revelation (*Commentarius in Apocalypsin*). Living so long after Augustine, he can be called "Augustine's student" only in a broad sense for having made much use of Augustine's *City of God* in his commentary.

12. Upon Erasmus's 1516 edition of the works of Jerome, a collection of commentaries on the thirteen letters of Paul circulated under Jerome's name, though even then his authorship was doubted. In 1693 Richard Simon made the conjecture that they were by Pelagius him-

when they interpret the passage we have cited. Nor do they take *faith* in any but the common meaning. But we shall discuss what the other Fathers taught and thought about the topic when we come to it.[13]

self, but the case was not proven until Alexander Souter did so in the third decade of the twentieth century. See Alexander Souter, *Pelagius's Expositions of the Thirteen Epistles of Paul*, 3 vols. (Cambridge: Cambridge University Press, 1922–31).

13. Romans 1558, London 1576, and Zürich 1580 have this last sentence. Heidelberg 1603 *om.* Coincidentally, neither does Marten, the first English translator of the *Common Places*.

[CHAPTER 11:
CONCLUDING REMARKS]

23. But for the time being, to come to the heart of the debate, we maintain that it is abundantly clear in Scripture that the works of unbelievers are sins. To defend this position not only did Augustine square off against Julian, but Ambrose did as well in *De vocatione gentium* 3,[1] where he says that absent the worship of the true God, what appear to be virtues are sins.[2] In *On Baptism* 2.7 Basil directly brings up this issue, and is on our side.[3] He cites passages from Scripture: from Isaiah, "When a sinner sacrifices, he might as well be slaying a dog, and when he offers fine

---

1. During the Reformation the *De vocatione gentium* was often believed to be by Ambrose, but it has since become clear that it was composed by Prosper of Aquitaine. See St. Prosper of Aquitaine, *The Call of All Nations*, trans. P. de Letter (Westminster, MD: Newman Press, 1952), 7.

2. St. Prosper of Aquitaine, *The Call of All Nations*, 28–30. Vermigli's reference here to Book 3 is puzzling, as the work only has two books, and the reference appears to be to Book 1, Chapter 4.

3. Basil, *De Baptismo* 2.7.

flour, he might as well be offering up the flesh of pigs" [66:3]. He adds, "The one who commits a sin is slave to sin and serves it alone" [John 8:34]. Also, "Nobody can serve two masters, God and Mammon" [Matt. 6:24]. Also, "What do the light and darkness, God and Belial, have to do with each other?" [2 Cor. 6:14] Finally, he cites the passage that we spoke on at length a little earlier, "A bad tree cannot produce good fruit" [Matt. 7:18]. From all these passages he concludes the very thing we teach.

I think it is now quite clear from what has been said what one is to think concerning the condition of people not yet regenerate: first, they are free from coercion. Next, they are able to do many things in accord with their free judgment in moral and civil actions. Finally, they enjoy some choice among sins themselves and now take up this sin, now that one, as they so choose. However, their freedom does not extend to doing the things that please God. Also, they are subject, whether they like it or not, to the hardships and catastrophes of this life.

[CHAPTER 12:
THE FREER WILL
OF THE REGENERATE]

Now we must discuss the freedom of people who are regenerate. It goes without saying that their freedom is not
less than the freedom we have said the ungodly have and
is actually superior in that it can rise up to good works
that are pleasing to God. Who does not know that what
Abraham did when he was prepared to sacrifice his son
was thoroughly pleasing to God? He was commended for
it with praise from God's own voice [Gen. 22]. Paul in
Philippians calls their almsgiving "sweet-smelling offerings" [Phil. 4:18] and in Hebrews we are taught that God
delights wonderfully in such offerings [Heb. 13:16]. And
this is the reason why Paul tells the Philippians to work
out their own salvation with fear and trembling [Phil.
2:12]. Yet what need is there for other passages, when the
Judge himself on the last day is going to review the good
works that godly men have conferred on the members of
Christ? And so since regenerate individuals are good trees,

it stands to reason that they should be able to produce, and do produce, good fruit.

However, those who have been born again ought never to forget that they have not acquired this freedom by their own merits, but rather by God's kindness. He refashioned them and in place of a heart of stone put a heart of flesh in them. They have their heavenly Father, not themselves, to thank for their being drawn to Christ. Unless they had been inwardly convinced in their minds through God the Father's powerful might, they would have fled from Christ no less than the others. Thus our minds are, as they say, passive with respect to the first transformation, or impression, of the Holy Spirit, yet after we are convinced and transformed, we are restored to being able to cooperate with grace and the Holy Spirit.

24. How this restoration of the will takes place must be considered under two headings. When at the beginning we described the nature of the will we made the prefatory remark that every error and every sin in judgment proceed from these two reasons: namely, because we are either completely ignorant about what is and what is not just when we deliberate about a thing, or because desire and emotion insert themselves, even when it is clear what is and is not just, and cause by their imposing presence less compelling reasons to be preferred to strong and weighty ones, and thus knowledge of what is right does not prevail.[1] The strength of the affections and all the mind's focus are concentrated on the reasons that argue for pleasures and desire, and the more virtuous arguments are dismissed and not put into effect. But due to regeneration, help is pro-

---

1. See section 1 above.

vided against both predicaments. As far as the first one is concerned, the light of faith is at hand, which applies the rule of God's law and so clearly perceives what is just and unjust in the actions we do. Secondly, although all the depravity of our affections is not completely taken away by the strength of the Holy Spirit, it is broken and weakened by it and cannot present so much of an obstacle to right judgment as it did before.

But since desire cannot be completely abolished as long as we live here on earth, the freedom granted to the godly to do the things that are pleasing to God is not complete or fully actualized, but weak and maimed, and is depicted as such in Scripture. The godly[2] in many ways are forcibly prevented from performing works that are pleasing to God as they would otherwise wish and as the law demands. They always feel a law in their members that fights against the law of their mind, whether they like it or not, and are carried away captive to the law of sin. As it is written in Galatians, "The flesh lusts against the Spirit so that they do not do what they want" [Gal. 5:17]. We also hear Paul complain that he does not do the good that he greatly desires, but instead does the evil he hates. While in their minds the godly *do* serve the law of God, and in their flesh the law of sin, they bear within themselves this significant gift from God: they deeply grieve and lament these obstacles and although they do not doubt they have the first fruits of the Spirit, they still groan and passionately long for complete restoration. Moreover,

----

2. Marten, *The Common Places* (London: Denham/Middleton, 1583), says "many men" here for *sancti* in all the Latin editions.

misdeeds befall[3] them daily and remind us how weak our freedom is. And so John says, "If we say we do not have sin, we deceive ourselves and the truth is not in us" [1 John 1:10]. James likewise says, "We all stumble in many ways" [James 3:2]. The Lord has taught us in daily prayer to cry unto the Father, "Forgive us our debts" [Matt. 6:12].

However, the paltriness of our freedom does not prevent us from cooperating with God and the Holy Spirit, making ourselves, as it were, suitable instruments. Accordingly, Paul admonished Timothy to fan the grace he had in himself [2 Tim. 1:6], and in his first letter to the Corinthians he instructed them to be zealous for the charismata and gifts that were better, as though their effort were required for them to be able to use one gift of the Spirit more so than another [1 Cor. 14:1]. But the ones who are said to have these things are simply mere men; since they have the grace and Spirit of God they are now called men of God, and because they are men of God they are said to be perfect and equipped for every good work. Accordingly, we grant that those who are born again in Christ have all the freedom that we granted to the ungodly, and moreover are able to perform works that are pleasing to God, though they are not exempt from either sin or the catastrophes or hardships of this life.

---

3. This is an interesting way to say that the godly sin every day, namely, that "misdeeds befall them daily" (*accidunt illis quotidiani lapsus*). Vermigli clearly wishes to underscore an element of passivity in the sins the regenerate commit.

Now would be the time to discuss the fourth condition of man,[4] but on this topic we can make a succinct response: since we are going to enjoy perfect happiness in our heavenly home, there is no kind of freedom that can be missed there (unless one wishes to call being able to sin and defecting from God, that is, the highest good, *freedom*). And since this is the highest form of freedom, we anticipate that in our heavenly home we shall be absolutely free.

---

4. See section 2 above for the four states into which Vermigli, following Augustine, divides the human will.

[CHAPTER 13: IS THE INBORN PROPENSITY TO SIN SIN?]

25. But now another question must be discussed: are the desire[1] and the depraved affections that remain in those born again sins, and should be spoken of as such? They are called by Paul *the law of sin* and *the law of our members*, and he has taught us that they remain in the godly after regeneration by his own example. Now, we cannot determine whether or not these are sins unless we understand what sin is beforehand. Augustine says sin is a thing said, done, or desired contrary to the law of God.[2] Yet on account of the ambiguity of the word *desired*, it is unclear whether this definition fits *all* sins or only the ones that are commonly called *actual*. If it refers to the full assent

---

1. Vermigli's word here is *concupiscentia*. For Vermigli's understanding of *concupiscence* and his treatment of it, see the first volume of this series: Peter Martyr Vermigli, *On Original Sin*, trans. Kirk Summers (Landrum, SC: Davenant Press, 2019), xviii.

2. Vermigli here cites Augustine (*Reply to Faustus*, *NPNF* 1/4:283) second-hand through Peter Lombard, *Sent.* 2.35.

of the will by which we give our assent to wicked desires, the definition is restricted to actual sins. On the other hand, if *desired* is taken as broadly and extensively as the last commandment, "Thou shalt not covet" [Exodus 20:17], the definition can be universal and encompass *all* sins. The teacher of the *Sentences*, book two, distinction thirty-five, cited the definition when he had already discussed original sin in depth and had moved on to examine the nature of the other sins, and so it appears he thought that that definition only pertained to *actual* sins. But whatever the case is, I am not going to discuss this matter at length. In *De paradiso* 8 Ambrose suggested an admittedly broad definition of sin:[3] "Sin is nothing but a transgression of God's law and disobedience to the divine commandments."[4] But disregarding the pronouncements of the Fathers, we should refer the matter to the reckoning of Scripture in order to ascertain clearly from it what sin is.

In chapter 3 of his first letter, John says, "Sin is ἀνομία" (that is, injustice) [1 John 3:4]. The Greek word is a compound of alpha privative and νόμος (*law*). Here the nature of sin is elegantly revealed: it is said to be a privation, in which something good is taken away from one who ought to possess it. If you ask what that good that is taken away through sin is, the Greek word νόμος (*law*)

---

3. Romans 1558, Zürich 1580, and Heidelberg 1603: *peccati*. London 1576: *non peccati*. London's reading is here obviously an error.

4. Ambrose, *De paradiso* 8 (*CSEL* 32:296). The exact quote runs: *quid est enim peccatum nisi praevaricatio legis divinae et caelestium inoboedientia praeceptorum.* Here one sees the sometimes approximate nature of Vermigli's quotations.

explains it: the good thing that is prescribed in God's *law* is taken away. And so, we can say that sin is *whatever is in opposition to God's law*.

Now we must consider whether or not this definition that we have taken from Scripture corresponds to the wickedness that remains in the saints after regeneration. On this question we answer in the affirmative, our opponents in the negative. Holy Scripture is incontrovertibly on our side. Paul clearly says that *the law of our members* wars against *the law of God* and our mind and the wisdom of the flesh are in enmity against God and neither submit to God's law nor can submit. The law of our members also opposes in every way the first and greatest commandment, "You shall love the LORD your God with all your mind, with all your heart, with all your strength" [Matt. 22:37]. If all our strength and faculties submitted to God, as they ought, this desire would nowhere be found in us. Furthermore, this same desire is at odds with the last commandment, "You shall not covet" [Exodus 20:17], and Augustine, as our multiple citations of him above point out, attests that these two commandments cannot be kept fully as long as we live this life. (He gives splendid reasons as to why these commandments have been given when they cannot be kept, reasons that I need not repeat here.)

26. We have shown on the basis of definition that the desire we are speaking about *is* sin. Now let us look at other arguments. One will be taken from the creation of man. Man was made in the image and likeness of God, and we have been predestined to be conformed to the image of the Son of God. We are also told to put on the new man who, as Paul says in Colossians 3, is being

renewed unto the knowledge and image of him who created him [v. 10]. This new man, as it says in Ephesians, is composed of true righteousness and holiness [4:24]. The image of God that we are told to put on means, as Tertullian says, we have the same affections and thoughts as God. Likewise, Paul exhorts us in Philippians to have the same mind as Christ [Phil. 2:5]. These affections and desires, however, grossly erase and blot out the image of God in us. Furthermore, what we are supposed to crucify, mortify, and put off must necessarily be sin since, if they were good, the Holy Spirit would instead tell us to develop them. But in Colossians Paul says, "Mortify your members that are earthly" [3:5], and in Galatians, "Those who belong to Christ have crucified their flesh with its desires" [5:24], and in another place, "Put off the old man" [Eph. 4:12]. If these affections are displeasing to God, that can be for no other reason than because they are sins. God is so forbearing that nothing displeases him except sin.

Finally, death is owed to sin as its wages; therefore, it cannot be present where there is not any sin. It only fell to the Son of God to undergo death while innocent, since he died because of our sins. We, on the other hand, die because we are not without sin. This being the case, let our opponents now explain why infants who have already been reborn in Christ, die, since they do not have actual sins and the guilt of original sin has been taken away. Only the desire and corruption of their nature, which has not been completely rectified, remain, as well as the wicked affections which Augustine in *Confessions* 11 says are found in infants, and confesses and condemns them as sins.[5] Therefore, since they are sins they not un-justly die because of them.

---

5. Augustine, *Confessiones* 11 (*Confessions*, *NPNF* 1/1:163–75). Book 11 does not discuss this topic at any length. A more likely place is Book 1.7–12 (*NPNF* 1/1:4648).

[CHAPTER 14:
CLASSES OF SIN & WHAT
CONSTITUTES ACTUAL SIN]

Since there are compelling reasons to demonstrate that the evil desires that remain in us after baptism are sins, it remains to see what class they belong to. Sin is generally distinguished as that which can be forgiven and that which cannot. The violation of God's law that is never forgiven is sin against the Holy Spirit. But where sin *can* be forgiven, that happens in two ways: it is either forgiven with the requirement of departing from it for good, which we see to be the case with the more serious sins that Paul says separate us from the kingdom of God and are commonly called *mortal*; or they are forgiven and we do not depart from them, partly because of our innate ignorance and partly because of the weakness we suffer from. These sins are called *less significant* and *venial*, and human life cannot be lived free of them. As we noted above, Paul made an elegant distinction between these sins when he exhorted us not to let[1] sin *reign* in us. And it was about this third

---

1. Romans 1558, Zürich 1580, and Heidelberg 1603: *sineremus*. Lon-

class of sins that the same Apostle complained when he said, "Miserable man that I am! Who will free me from this body of death?" [Rom. 7:24].

It is about these sins that our theologians are thinking about when they teach that people's works, however holy the people may be, are not without mortal[2] sin, since we perform nothing that is free from flaws of this sort, which are called mortal because by their nature they merit death, since the wages of sin is death, and also because we are unable to enjoy eternal life as long as we carry around these imperfections with us. We are shut off from it until we in death put off all corruption. Moreover, it is written, "Cursed is he who does not abide by everything that is written in the words of this law" [Gal. 3:10]. And whoever laments with Paul that he does not do the good he would want to do, does not perform everything that the law demands, and so is not entirely exempt from the curse, even though by God's mercy it is not imputed to him unto eternal perdition.

27. Thus do our theologians speak about the good works of godly people, not because they deny good works or think that, when done by regenerate persons, they are not pleasing to God, but in order to acknowledge our uncleanness and impurity, which we are insensate and beyond blind in recognizing. Besides the sin against the Holy Spirit, which we can set aside, the other sins are classed ac-

---

don 1576: *sinerimus*, a clear error.

2. Vermigli evidently means that Protestant theologians made the point that even the traditionally dubbed "venial" sins were "mortal," in the sense that they were no less sins than the so-called "mortal" sins of the Roman Catholic Church, because they merited death equally.

cording to three phases. In the first is innate desire. From it continuously emanate in the second phase the initial affections and impulses toward various misdeeds. In the third phase the assent of the will enters into it and issues forth in action. Paul marked out these three phases when he said, "Let sin not reign in your mortal bodies so as to obey its desires" [Rom. 6:12]. The sin which should not be allowed to reign is our innate desire and natural depravity. The initial affections are the desires that the former gives birth to. Them we are told not to obey. Then comes obedience which completes and perfects the sin, which is commonly called *actual*. Obviously, natural depravity refers to original sin. Likewise, sin that receives the assent of the will is called *actual*.

The question is concerning the initial affections; namely, whether they are to be referred to original or actual sin (although because of Christ they do not bind us to new guilt and the necessity of undergoing the judgment of God). They are at any rate intermediate and share in both groups. Insofar as we do desire or long for something through them, they possess an element of actual sin, and Paul uses the verbs *to do* (ποιεῖν) and *to practice* (πράσσειν), which clearly indicate some sort of action. On the other hand, they have in common with original sin, which is not undertaken deliberately and willfully, the fact that we experience affections of this sort against our will.

Commenting on Matthew 7, Jerome draws a distinction between *emotion* (πάθος) and *preliminary emotion* (προπάθεια).[3] He says the initial affections are an *emotion*

---

3. This idea is attributed to Jerome in the *Catena Aurea* but does not appear to occur in the existing MSS of his commentary on Matthew.

(πάθος) after they have received the consent of the will, but are a *preliminary emotion* (προπάθεια) when at the beginning they stir and goad one on. He goes on to say that although the *preliminary emotions* are blameworthy, they are not regarded as an offense, while an *emotion* is regarded as sin. Note here that Jerome admits that the initial affections *do* have the *guilt* (*culpa*) of sin, but that that guilt is free of the *charge* (*crimen*) of sin, that is, thanks to Christ it is not imputed unto death or is not regarded as an offense from a human perspective. And further, since sin is commonly classed as that which is *only* sin and that which is *both* sin and the penalty of sin—Augustine mentions this distinction when commenting on Psalm 57.[4] He says that the original apostasy from God was only sin, while what follows is both sin and the penalty of sin up until man reaches Hell. Whatever evils then are committed between the original apostasy and Hell are not only sins, but punishments as well exacted for other sins. Paul has shown this very well in Romans. He says first that, while the pagans knew God, they did not glorify him as God. He then adds that they were given over to their depraved desires, being full of all malice, greed, etc. [Rom. 1:21–24]. Lastly, he mentions Hell's damnation, "But you according to your hardness and unrepentant heart store up for yourself wrath on the day of wrath and the revelation of God's righteous judgment, when he shall render to each according to his works" [Rom. 2:5].

See Thomas Aquinas, *Catena Aurea: Commentary on the Four Gospels*, trans. Mark Pattison (Oxford: J. Parker, 1874), 185.

4. Augustine, *Enarrationes in psalmos* 57 (*Expositions on the Psalms*, *NPNF* 1/8:229–36).

And yet there are many who do not think that these sins are the penalty of sin on the grounds that people derive a good amount of pleasure from them. Yet were they not blind they would clearly understand the Apostle that these are punishments, and severe ones at that. He says their hearts were blinded and they themselves rendered foolish, even though they claimed to be wise, and were handed over by God to a reprobate mind so that they would abuse their bodies [Rom. 1:22]. What is this if not the severest punishment? If somebody's hands were at once cut off or eyes ripped out after he had committed theft, we would say that he had been severely punished by a divine power. Paul says that these people were deprived of their mind, that their hearts were made senseless, that their bodies disgracefully defiled, and this is not considered to be punishment? How can we expect our minds to be safe, sound, undefiled if sin reigns in it? Solomon says, "Will one cherish fire in his bosom and not burn his clothes? Or will one walk over hot coals and not scorch his feet?" [Prov. 6:27]. Sin is said to be a penalty because it injures and debases our nature. The depravity of original sin has so marred it that it can now scarcely be thought of as half-alive, and the depraved affections and impulses that periodically arise from it render it stronger, unless they are beaten back and mortified. If you give in to them they become ever more powerful, and thus our nature continuously hurtles downward.

28. The point of all this is for us to understand that the innate desire and depraved affections that still remain in our minds belong to this class of sins.[5] Not only that,

---

5. I.e., actual.

but they are also the penalty of another antecedent sin, namely original sin (if not some other more serious one). One should note that original apostasy is also a sin that doubles as a penalty, since as we have said there is no sin that does not do the most appalling damage to man's nature, and thus at least contains within itself the penalty due to itself. But not every sin is the penalty of another antecedent sin. On the other hand, the sins that we are now treating we contend are the penalties for a preceding sin, and maintain that they are also sins.

[CHAPTER 15: IMPLICATIONS OF THIS POSITION]

Yet it seems puzzling to many how they can be sins when they are necessary. On this question let us listen to Augustine in *On Free Will* 3.18:

> Even those things that are done by necessity are condemnable, as when an individual wishes to do good, yet is unable. For were it not the case, how do we explain the statements, "The good I want to do I do not do; instead, the evil I do not want is what I do" [Rom. 7:15], and "To will the good is at my disposal, but the means to carry it out I do not find" [Rom. 7:18], and "The flesh lusts against the spirit and the spirit against the flesh" [Gal. 5:17]. For since these two are opposed to each other, you do not do the things you want. But all this is the common lot of man and results from the original condemnation to death. If this is not man's penalty, but his nature, then these are not sins, since if there is no devia-

tion from the way man was originally created so as to be unable to be better, in committing these sins he does what he is expected to do. If man were good, it would be different. As it is, because the matter stands so, he is not good and does not have it in his power to be good, either because he does not see how he ought to be or because he sees, yet is unable to be the way he sees he should be. That that is a penalty who would question?[1]

So Augustine. In these words there is much that is worthy of attention. First, he states that many things that one necessarily experiences are condemnable. Secondly, he gives a reason as to why they are called sins: because they represent a departure from the way we were originally created. Thirdly, he says man is not good and does not have it in his power to be good. Fourthly, he gives a two-fold reason as to why he is unable to be good: either because he does not see what he should do or sees, but, due to his powerlessness, cannot execute it. Finally, note that he understands these points to refer to born again individuals. He cites the words of Paul in Galatians, as well as the passages that we just produced, which we have shown can only be taken to refer to the born again. However, what Jerome writes in his *Interpretation of the Faith*, "We maintain that those who with the Manicheans say man is unable to avoid evil are in error," appears to be at odds with this statement of Augustine's.[2]

---

1. Augustine, *De libero arbitrio* 3.18.

2. And rightly so, nor does Vermigli need to reconcile the two, as he

29. Yet these statements can be reconciled with little difficulty. Jerome speaks of nature as it was created by God and writes against the Manicheans who taught that we cannot resist sin because we were created naturally evil by an evil god. Now, none of us doubts that when he was first created, man was perfectly free. On the other hand, that Augustine is speaking of our *fallen* nature is quite clear from his saying, "These things belong to men and result from his condemnation to death." He then states that this is fallen man's penalty. Furthermore, if these sins refer to those who are born again, we can say that Jerome's statement only pertains to the grosser vices that separate us from the kingdom of God and that those reborn in Christ are able to abstain from, while Augustine speaks in the broadest of terms and understands by *sins* those that we are currently discussing, which we cannot live free of in this life. In fact, this latter solution is cited by the teacher of the *Sentences*, book two, distinction thirty-six.[3]

But they will object and say to us that injury is done to baptism if we say that sin is not removed through it. But we cannot rightly be charged on this count, since we do affirm that the *guilt* of our sins is removed through regeneration. Even though these vices remain, as both Scripture teaches and experience attests, their liability and guilt are

---

attempts below. The reference comes from Peter Lombard (*Sentences* 2.36.6), who attributes this saying to Jerome in the latter's *Symboli explanation ad Damasum*, but in reality the statement belongs to Pelagius who made it in his *Epistola ad Innocentium I* (see Migne, *PL* 48:488, 610).

3. Peter Lombard, *Sentences* 2.36.

removed. For this reason Augustine says several times[4] that while desire remains, its guilt has been taken away through Christ. He adds that sometimes the act and work of sin are absent (as we see in the case of theft and adultery), while the guilt still remains; and that sometimes guilt is removed, while the sin remains, which is quite clear in the case of the desire we are talking about. The desire abides, yet we cannot be condemned on account of it to eternal death.

If you ask why it is called *sin* when its guilt has been removed, I answer, that it is not imputed to us does not issue from its own nature. As far as its nature is concerned, it deserves death and condemnation, as we have shown above; exemption from its being imputed to us, on the other hand, comes from somewhere else, namely, Christ's mercy. Any and everything has to be assessed by itself and its nature. And so, since the defining characteristic of sin is to fight against God's law, and we see this take place in our desire and initial affections, they have to be called sins. And this position of ours does not cause us to fall into the absurdity of which the Pelagians accused Augustine and other catholics, as though they were saying sin is not erased, but shaved off, through regeneration, in that when hairs are shaved off, the roots from which they grow again still remain. Although we maintain that our desire and depraved affections remain in those who are reborn, we also maintain that God has been completely reconciled to us. And so, although on the basis of their nature they are sins, they are nullified so as not to be imputed to us any longer.

---

4. E.g., *Contra Iulianum* 4.17.51–52.

Therefore, from the point of view of imputation, absolutely nothing of those sins remains.

30. Finally, they protest that we do violence to Augustine in saying that he asserts these to be sins when, in interpreting himself, he shows that he did not call it sin in the strict sense of the word. For just as writing is called a *hand* because it is produced by the hand, so these are called sins because they result from original sin; and just as cold is called *slow* because it makes us slow, so these are called sins because they provoke us to sins, yet strictly speaking are not sins. They say Augustine not only interpreted his calling them sins in this way, but also provided us with the way we should be understanding Paul when *he* calls them sins. To this we respond: first, if Augustine or anyone else of the Fathers says these are not sins, we should understand that in terms of comparison, insofar as they are compared to *actual* sins, yet the nature of sin cannot essentially be eliminated from them. Arguing this in the clearest of terms in another passage, Augustine says in *Against Julian* 6.8, "There is indeed iniquity present when in one person either what is higher is disgracefully subservient to what is lower or what is lower disgracefully resists what is higher, even if they are not permitted to get the upper hand."[5] In calling this sin *iniquity* he clearly shows that the character of sin we set forth above belongs to it.

In *Against Julian* 5.3 he also writes, "The lust of the flesh against which the good spirit desires is sin because it contains within itself disobedience against the mind's direction; it is the penalty of sin because it is the conse-

---

5. Actually, Augustine, *Contra Iulianum* 6.19 (*Fathers of the Church*, 35:374).

97

quence of what one who is in disobedience deserves; and it is the cause of sin due to dereliction on the part of the one who consents to it."[6] Here you see Augustine call lust *sin* in three ways, nor can one say that he writes these things about an unregenerate person, since he expressly says, "against which the good spirit desires," and the spirit of God that resists the desires is not found in the ungodly. Therefore, we have from Augustine three passages: one which we cited above from book five of *On Free Will*, and two from *Against Julian*.[7] In these passages he clearly states that this desire is a sin, and gives the reason why he thinks so. And, as far as the interpretation of Paul is concerned, our opponents ought not to seek a defense in figurative language and say that this should not be called *sin* in the strict sense of the word, seeing that proof is provided from both Paul and other places in Scripture as to why this desire is correctly and properly called *sin*. It is astonishing that at other times these men are so inclined towards figurative interpretations, when in the case of one particular statement, "This is my body"—a case where figurative interpretation best fits—they so vehemently object to every species of it! If one wants other passages from the Fathers where this desire is shown to be a sin, we have cit-

6. Augustine, *Contra Iulianum* 5.3 (*Fathers of the Church*, 35:249).

7. The two references to Augustine's *Against Julian* are clear. However, Vermigli does not cite Book 5 of Augustine's *On Free Will* in this portion of the *Loci*. Either the reference occurs in the original commentary on Romans (which is doubtful, since neither in that work is there any reference to Book 5 anywhere near the present passage), or Vermigli here means Book 3, which he cites a few pages above. The latter option is more likely.

ed Jerome's commentary on Matthew above, and there are a great many other pronouncements from other ancient Fathers found cited in Augustine's *Against Julian* which all support us.

[What follows is copied from a relevant discussion towards the end of Chapter 2 of Vermigli's commentary on 1 Corinthians.8]

31. Now we must explore whether or not freedom of will has been entirely lost on the basis of what we have discussed from the beginning. In asserting that the natural man can in no way recognize the things of God, Paul appears for a moment to challenge free will, since if we do not have the means to perceive spiritual things through our natural ability, how will we ever actualize that ability in our actions, seeing that we meet with much more difficulty and resistance in our actions than in our understanding?

Nor is this the only thing that appears to present an obstacle. The predestination, or foreknowledge, of God does as well. It seems to be possible to conclude that if God knows everything before it happens, and he cannot err, freedom of will vanishes and everything happens by necessity.

Divine power by which everything comes to pass also presents no small difficulty here, since God's will is so ef-

---

8. As the title indicates, this section was taken from Vermigli, *In selectissimam S. Pauli priorem ad Corinthios epistolam* (Zürich: Froschauer, 1551), 58v–62v.

fectual that Paul says in Romans, "Who can oppose his will?" [9:19].

Furthermore, Scripture presents the power of sin as so great that practically everything in us has been ruined and corrupted through it. Consequently, the power that is left to a will so feeble cannot do what reason commands. What is more, so much stress is laid on the grace of Christ in Scripture that we are said apart from it to be unable to perform anything that is pleasing or acceptable to God. And since grace is not given equally to everybody, their freedom is considered undermined, since they do not have this grace in their power.

Astrologers also talk much about heavenly forces and argue that somehow everything that happens to us depends on them, so that there does not seem to be left any use of absolute freedom regarding future occurrences. Finally, there have been those who maintained that things that will happen have definite causes which being so interconnected and inextricably intertwined virtually imply necessity or inescapable fate.

32. We need not dwell much on the argument from our intellective ability since it has been clearly shown from what we have said so far that, as far as works that are truly good and pleasing to God are concerned, we must not posit such freedom in those who are not yet reborn. And so this line of reasoning should not be dismissed as false as it firmly supports the Apostle's teaching.

[CHAPTER 16:
FREEDOM OF WILL AND
GOD'S FOREKNOWLEDGE]

There is more of a problem and difficulty in the next idea, since few are able to see how God's providence, or fore-knowledge (to use their language) allows any freedom to remain in our will. So thorny and tricky is this topic that some of the ancient writers went so far in this line of rea-soning as to conclude that there arises an absolute necessi-ty in our actions; in fact, they hold God himself to be con-strained by this necessity. Accordingly, a common proverb was bandied about to the effect that necessity is for God himself inescapable, and he dares nothing against it.[1] Tak-ing advantage of their license, the poets went further and said that many things even happen against the will of the gods. Homer portrayed Zeus as sad and lamenting the ne-cessity of fate by whose power he was not permitted to save Sarpedon, his dear and beloved son, from imminent

---

1. Cf. Simonides's dictum, "Not even the gods resist necessity" (ἀνάγκη δ' οὐδὲ θεοὶ μάχονται) (Plato, *Protagoras* 345d).

death.[2] Homer also depicts Poseidon as indignant over the death of his son, the Cyclops.[3] Driven by desire for revenge, he would have kept Odysseus away from home indefinitely, and complains how doing so is outright denied him by the Fates. In Vergil Juno complains just as furiously that she waged war for so many years together with one nation, yet is unable to drive the Trojan fleet from Italy as she had desired.[4]

However, we Christians do not speak this way about God. We are unmistakably taught by Scripture that "nothing is impossible for God" [Luke 1:37] and from Christ himself we have learned that "for God all things are possible" [Matt. 19:26]. Moreover, after the example of Abraham our faith rests above all on the conviction that God can deliver on whatever he promises. Nor should we entertain the thought that Christ was either condemned to die or driven to the cross against the will and desire of the Father. God willed these things to happen; he was not induced by inescapable necessity, but by an overflowing and superabundant love for mankind. Thus Scripture teaches us. It says, "God so loved the world that he gave his Son," etc. [John 3:16]. It is also written in Romans, "He who did not spare his own Son, but gave him up for us all" [Rom. 8:32]. Christ himself was driven by the same love to die for us, and taught that no one has a greater love than that he should lay down his life for his friends [John 15:13], then showed that he exceeded the bounds of human love

---

2. *Iliad* 16.433–34.

3. *Odyssey* 1.20.

4. *Aeneid* 1.34–49.

in wishing to die for his enemies! And just how willingly and voluntarily he underwent death he clearly showed in the last supper he held with his apostles in accordance with Passover custom when he says, "I have greatly desired to eat this Passover with you" [Luke 22:15].

33. We consequently see that the Lord's death was foreseen and foreknown and did not do any violence whatsoever either to Christ's or the Father's will. For this reason Cicero, an otherwise thoroughly erudite man, is quite surprising. Augustine argues with him quite heatedly regarding this issue in *City of God* 5.9 (and 10 in particular).[5] The debate stems from the fact that in book two of *On Divination* everything that his brother Quintus adduced in the previous book is refuted, and Cicero is intent upon using every means to subvert predictions about the future and God's foreknowledge. Accordingly, Augustine asserts that astrologers hold views that are much more bearable because, while they attribute too much to the stars, they have not altogether done away with divination and foreknowledge. As Augustine also relates in his *Confessions*, there was a physician who was a very sober-minded individual and loathed astrology.[6] When he was asked how it turned out that astrologers made so many true predictions, he did not venture to discredit divination in its entirety in the face of all of history and experience, but responded that there was a kind of destiny diffused throughout the world, and it was not incredible, he suggested, if sentient minds perceived it in one way or another.

---

5. Augustine, *De civitate Dei* 5.9–10 (*City of God*, NPNF 1/2:90–92).

6. Augustine, *Confessiones* 4.3.5 (*Confessions*, NPNF 1/1:69–70).

Certainly there cannot be imagined anything more inconsistent than to assert on the one hand that God exists, but on the other deprive him of the knowledge of future events. The prophet Isaiah was so keen to have these statements coextensive that he said, "Proclaim to us the things that will be, and we will admit you are gods" [Isaiah 41:23]. The book Cicero wrote, *On the Nature of the Gods*, convinces one that he did not think well or consistently about God. Arguing here in the person of Cotta, he seeks to do away with God's nature completely. It is certainly a lamentable fact that so great a man fell afoul of what a psalm of David castigates the senseless for doing: "The fool has said in his heart, 'There is no God'" [Psalm 14:1]. I do not quite understand what he had in mind when he gave this role in the dialogue to Cotta, the *pontifex maximus*, unless he had in view the fact that, generally speaking, there is no group that speaks more loosely and thinks more poorly about God than those to whose care ceremonies and sacred things have been entrusted. After engaging in as lengthy a discussion as he saw fit, at the end of the book Cicero, being well aware that it is a very objectionable thing to put forth an opinion that denies God, comes out in favor of Lucius Balbus, while mentioning, however, that Cotta's view found favor with Velleius.

Cicero was not just interested in learning; he was particularly interested in politics as well. And so, since he believed that civilization would collapse if free will were taken away, and did not see how this freedom could be reconciled with foreknowledge of future events, he preferred to allow God to be deprived of his wisdom than our will its freedom. Here one can ascertain the darkness and blindness toward creation the first man's sin has hurled

the human race into! What sort of insanity is it to desire to dislodge God, the Creator of everything, from the
citadel of his knowledge so that you can preserve man?
This is that excessive love of oneself that Scripture everywhere condemns. We would rather everything perish than
ourselves. This is not what godliness urges. Therefore, we
who are taught by the Divine Spirit say that both are to
be asserted: God foreknows everything *and* our freedom
of will is retained,[7] as we showed above. This is the way
Scripture teaches us. We read: "Those whom he foreknew
he predestined to be conformed to the image of his Son"
[Rom. 8:10]. We have also learned from Scripture that we
were chosen by God before the foundation of the world,
that the hairs of our head are numbered down to the last
one, and that sparrows do not fall apart from the will of
our exalted Father. Since we also believe that God does
everything rightly and justly, we cannot suppose him to
act without reason and intelligence.

34. But, come, let us take a closer look at Cicero's
argumentation. He says:

---

7. Vermigli's language here can be confusing, not to mention the fact
that the present section comes from a different commentary than previous sections. He now denies free will and now asserts it, but in two
different senses. He asserts we do have free will in the sense that we
are not automatons doing whatever God decrees, even to the point
of his actively decreeing our sinning, which is an unthinkable thing
(section 39), but that we choose the evil we do freely and willfully.
Yet, though we are not coerced by God to sin, we do sin *necessarily*,
as Vermigli explains in Section 5, and so in this sense Vermigli denies
freedom of will.

If the future is foreknown, occurrences will be in a definite configuration vis-à-vis each other and, since nothing happens without a cause, one will necessarily grant a configuration and relationship of causes. Thus it will follow that everything that is done will be done out of necessity. Accordingly, just and beneficial laws will vanish, there will be no reason for advice or criticism, and no place for religion or prayer. Therefore, you have to choose which of the two you prefer: to preserve either divination and God's foreknowledge or the free operation of the human will. One cannot have both at the same time.[8]

They are inconsistent, he believes. Therefore, he thinks it is absolutely necessary to defend and advocate for one of the two positions, while rejecting as false and harmful the other. As Augustine said with as much acumen as he did reverence, in posing this dilemma, Cicero, an otherwise thoroughly intelligent man who wants to make us free, *actually* makes us sacrilegious because we rob God of his knowledge of future events. One should be careful to note that his arguments fly in the face of the predictions of our prophets no less than running counter to the pagan practices of divination which Cicero was then discussing. For this reason we think we should parry his close argumentation thus: let it be granted to him as he wishes, that

---

8. Although Vermigli introduces this passage as quoted direct speech, it is not found in the extant works of Cicero. It bears some similarity with *De natura deorum* 1.1, but the argument there is somewhat different.

to establish God's foreknowledge there is with God a determined and definite configuration of both occurrences and causes. But we deny the final inference he draws, that therefore everything will happen by necessity. For, even if a definite configuration of causes is established, it does not follow that there cannot be found among those causes some that are able to retain their freedom (or, as they say, their contingency). It appears that Cicero makes here a greater mistake than the Stoics. So that man's freedom is left intact, Cicero wants to remove all configuration of causes and completely do away with predicting the future, things that are so much a part of God's nature that deprived of them it cannot subsist. The Stoics, on the other hand, in order not to detract anything from the divine nature introduce their notion of fate, and so that there may be a place for our intact and unimpaired will they removed it entirely from their arrangement of interconnected causes.

35. But we must square off with him closely here in order to give a solid defense of the fact that God's knowledge does not present any obstacle to our will, even though the former encompasses the future. The human will never realizes anything but what God foreknows and wills it to realize. When he foreknows that tomorrow I will run or read, to be sure, I will read and run, not compelled by any necessity, but rather, as they say, contingently. As far as I am concerned, I could have done either. If you press me and say, "You will nevertheless do what God knows you will do," I grant it, but it does not follow that I was not able to act otherwise, because we do not always do whatever we can; on the contrary, several things could be done that will in no way be done. The fact that I read or ran

resulted completely from my choice, because, if anything, willing and not willing lie within our power. And so, when they say, "Because God foreknew that you would read tomorrow, you will of necessity read," one must ask them in turn if by *necessity* they understand a will that is compelled and resistant. If this is what they mean, I deny outright that it follows, since it is possible that God foreknew that I would do something, and that I would do it willingly, not coerced or resistant. Now, if they hold it to be absolutely necessary that I have to do that, I do not object, since the issue now is not over a thing that is done or not done, but rather it is the manner and procedure we are discussing.

Nor are advice, laws, criticism, or the prayers of religion done away with, as Cicero thought. These will to be sure continue to have efficacy, more so than he would expect, because God does not just have mankind's salvation in his foreknowledge, but encompasses within his mind the ways and means by which he wills to help them. And so if we see a brother in need of the above mentioned remedies, let us make confident use of them. They will be beneficial to him as far as God foresaw and wills them to be. Nor ought we to stop performing our duty, although every mortal would perhaps assert that we are wasting our time, because we ought to follow the law that God has prescribed to us, not his secret foreknowledge regarding which we have no idea as to what decree he has made concerning the future. And since the foreknowledge of God does not have the same nature, or as they say, essence as our mind, we must pass judgment on actions that proceed from our mind as they ought to be conceptualized on the basis of the nature of our character and will, not on the basis of what lies outside of them. Therefore, since it is the essence of will not to do anything unwillingly or under coercion, it cannot be compelled from any outside source to do so. It would sooner be destroyed and cease to exist than to have any coerced action drawn out of it, just as you could get any of us to agree to not being human more easily than you could get us to agree to be human, yet without a rational soul, since no one can any longer be human the moment you introduce a soul bereft of reason.

36. Yet if one continues to ask whether or not it should be granted that I am going to necessarily read once God has foreknown it, I shall respond: a kind of necessity can be granted conditionally, or hypothetically, but not a thoroughgoing and absolute one, and so with this particular necessity I grant the free choice of the will can be perfectly compatible. In his *Ethics*, Aristotle discusses, and with great learning at that (as he always does), whether or not jettisoning things into the sea when a shipwreck is about to happen should be considered a voluntary act.[9] Although he says here that it is an action of sorts with both voluntariness and involuntariness, he concludes that actions of this sort belong in the voluntary class. The reason is that, for the time during which the sailors are in peril, they will and definitely choose the jettisoning. If a philosopher of his caliber did not think twice about placing voluntary action in actions of the sort where people experience a certain forceful compulsion to choose what they never would have done had they not been in that crisis, how much more will we refrain from removing the voluntary element from our regular and routine actions, seeing that we sense we are doing and desiring the things

---

9. Aristotle, *Nicomachean Ethics* 3.1 (1110a8–11).

that occur to us on our own accord and with a spirit that is as willing as can be, even though we do not deny that God long ago foreknew them?

Similarly, Chrysostom clearly shows that the sort of necessity we are hypothetically entertaining does not do away with the free operation of our will. When writing on this epistle,[10] he interpreted the words, "There must be heresies so that those of us who are genuine may be made apparent" [1 Cor. 11:19], in this way: "Christ did not speak in any different terms when he said, 'It is necessary that scandals happen. However, woe to the man through whom the scandal comes!'" [Matt. 18:7].[11] Likewise he said to the apostles, "It was necessary for the Christ to suffer and thus arrive at his glory" [Luke 24:26]. Even though they are called necessary, all these actions in Scripture are

---

10. I.e., 1 Corinthians.

11. The passage in Chrysostom reads: "By 'factions,' here he means those which concern not the doctrines, but these present divisions. But even if he had spoken of the doctrinal heresies, not even thus did he give them any handle. For Christ Himself said, 'it must needs be that occasions of stumbling come' (Matthew 18:7), not destroying the liberty of the will nor appointing any necessity and compulsion over man's life, but foretelling what would certainly ensue from the evil mind of men; which would take place, not because of his prediction, but because the incurably disposed are so minded. For not because he foretold them did these things happen: but because they were certainly about to happen, therefore he foretold them. Since, if the occasions of stumbling were of necessity and not of the mind of them that bring them in, it was superfluous his saying, 'Woe to that man by whom the occasion cometh.' But these things we discussed more at length when we were upon the passage itself; now we must proceed to what is before us" (*Homilies on First Corinthians*, NPNF 1/12:158).

to be explained in such a way as to detract nothing from the human will. The Scholastics typically call this kind of necessity *necessity of consequence* and not *necessity of the consequent.*

37. But a few individuals aver, "These distinctions clearly do us no good if what God has foreknown is absolutely going to happen." On the contrary, they offer no mean benefit! From them we realize that the human will is by no means coerced, but rather free and of its own volition desires whatever it wills. Otherwise, I ask you in turn, "Would you like to be saved against God's wishes and will?" I think not. Now, if you would like to be saved in accordance with his will, it must be that he is not ignorant of your salvation, since there is general agreement that nobody wishes what he does not know. We often have the chance to watch people playing a game with each other. We would not dream of saying that our onlooking and knowledge imposes any necessity on the players, and yet while we see them in their game they are necessarily playing. And so, just as this necessity does no violence to the nature of their will, so God's foreknowledge does not coerce man's judgment.

There are some who snap back and say that this analogy does not fit the question at hand. Nobody ever watches players who do not really exist and play, whereas it is hypothesized that God foreknew our actions from the beginning when neither we nor any actions on our part yet existed. To these I would say that everything is present to God no differently than those who play fall within the scope of the spectators.[12] Each person should therefore

---

12. That God enjoys an eternal present is an idea that goes back to

be careful not to throw back on God the causes of his own sins. Whenever such a thought occurs to his mind, he should consider his covetousness, lust, anger, hatred, as well as the other emotions of his spirit that he terribly suffers from and should look for the causes of his sins from these sources. Nor should much weight be given in this matter to the Aristotelians who deny that God perceives the individual and the isolated because they do not want it thought that they consider the divine mind to be mean and lowly if it derives its knowledge from perishable things. This does not follow from our teachings because we believe God has perfect knowledge concerning all things from himself and has no need of appropriating it from anywhere else.

----

the Christian philosopher Boethius in his *Consolation of Philosophy* V, prosa 6, who incorporated the idea in his vindication of man's free will.

[CHAPTER 17:
FREEDOM OF WILL AND GOD'S
POWER: CONCERNING ASTROLOGY]

38. The third point was that God's power is thought to be incompatible with our freedom. But this is neither cogent nor compelling. Whereas God does whatever he wishes with the extraordinary power he is endowed with, he leaves the conditions and natures of created things untouched and does not do violence to them or alter them in any way other than their condition allows. Thus it is said in the Book of Wisdom that God reaches mightily from end to end and disposes everything elegantly [8:1] (or as the Greek text has it, χρηστῶς, that is, beneficially). This could by no means be said if the nature of created things were altered by God's absolute power. In fine, in the administration of the world God here exercises his power to assign harmoniously to each thing its peculiar action.

The fourth point was that sin presents an obstacle to freedom of will on the grounds that it has so enfeebled human strength as to make it virtually powerless. At present there is no need for a long discussion of this topic. We have already abundantly shown in what has been said so far how our freedom has been impaired by sin, especially as it concerns actions that are truly and genuinely good, which are pleasing and acceptable to God, and it was demonstrated that our freedom has not been entirely abolished, but rather a good part of it still remains.

39. Concerning astrological influence there will be no need for a long discussion since the astronomers in their very own books state that the wise man will control the stars. If the thing they predicted were inescapable their entire livelihood would vanish, since nobody would be interested in buying knowledge about things he did not believe he could avoid or change with determined effort, which would of course result if they attributed absolute necessity to their predictions. Subsequently, prayer, piety, and all worship of the divine would disappear,[1] since who would pray to God to get anything if he were already convinced that it could not be granted to him? As Augustine was in the habit of saying, those who think this do Heaven a great wrong, since they believe that a senate has been established there to enjoin wicked acts of inescapable inevitability. If such a legislative body existed on earth its destruction would be called for. How much less is it to be believed that such a body is tolerated by God in Heaven? What room, tell me, will be left for judgment if we do everything under compulsion?

Some people get around this by saying that the heavens only indicate the things that will be, but do not de-

---

1. Romans 1558, Zürich 1580, and Heidelberg 1603: *auferretur*, which is what I have translated. London 1576: *auferetur*. The former is the better reading.

termine them by any necessity.[2] They produce the passage from Genesis where it seems to say that the stars are established as signs. But that passage should be taken as referring to seasons, winds, rainy weather, storms, and other such things. They will be hard put to prove how they can support their seeing in the heavens clear signs of future occurrences especially in the case of human actions. What can they say about twins who though conceived at the same moment under the same horoscope have allotted to them, as experience shows, entirely different circumstances? Augustine's *City of God* 5.2 is worth reading, where he writes that two brothers once turned out to be affected by such similar constitutions that when the one fell ill the other felt poorly as well, and when the one began to get better the other did too. When asked about this, Hippocrates replied that he thought they were twins and consequently had the same sort of physical makeup, while the astrologer Posidonius on the other hand attributed the entire thing to the stars, alleging that they had had the same horoscope when they were born. "But what," Augustine asks, "will these two men say about twins and a host of other creatures that, while born at the same hour and moment, experience an entirely different set of outcomes?"[3] Whereas Augustine says that he got this example from Cicero, we do not find it in his books unless he perhaps found it in his *On Fate*, a work we have in mutilated and completely tattered form.

---

2. Romans 1558, London 1576, and Zürich 1580: *non*. Heidelberg 1603: *nos*. The former is to be preferred.

3. Augustine, *De civitate Dei* 5.2 (*City of God*, NPNF 1/2:85–86).

40. Furthermore, the fate that the Stoics premised to have absolute necessity does not present us with any problem, since we do not make use of fate. They exempted the wills of individuals from it, believing that everything would collapse if they subsumed free will with the other causes under fate. Nevertheless, it appears that they did not entirely extricate man's will from fate except insofar as the first choice was concerned, which they wanted to be fixed squarely within our decision-making. However, whenever we choose an undertaking that falls under fate they held that all the things that are connected to it follow necessarily. It is as Euripides said of Laius, "He was free not to sire a child, but once he did he had to undergo the things that Apollo prophesied were fated."[4] But as I said above, I maintain that things are connected as God has ordained and foreknown them, yet leaving their nature and character unimpaired. Whatever ought to have contingency (as they say) has it, and whatever things for which it is appropriate to be constrained by necessity are indeed constrained by it. But, make no mistake, while grace has particularly been thought incompatible with free will, it does not do away with it, but in point of fact helps and restores it. However, we wish now to lay aside this topic so as not to engage in an investigation that is more hair-splitting than befits a Christian. Let each person follow his own calling, and let us cease inquiring too far into God's secret and hidden will, his foreknowledge and his predestination. Let us rather follow the knowledge about God that is lucidly set forth to us in Scripture.

---

4. Cf. Euripides, *Phoenician Women*, lines 18–20.

PETER MARTYR VERMIGLI: SECOND PART OF THE COMMON PLACES

THIRD CHAPTER
On the law

[CHAPTER 1:
THE LAW DEFINED]¹

1. Here I have thought it good to add a few things about the nature of the Law and at the same time to show how the Manicheans and Pelagians failed to understand it, as well as what it accomplishes in us both before regeneration and after we have been justified. To begin with, concerning its formal cause the same thing should be said that Paul said in this letter,² when he writes that it is spiritual.³ Its final cause, to draw people to an awareness of

---

1. This section is taken from the fifth chapter of Vermigli's commentary on Romans, *In epistolam S. Pauli ad Romanos commentarii* (Basil: Petrus Perna, 1558), 190–92.

2. I.e., Romans.

3. Aristotle held that we cannot truly know anything unless we can explain it with reference to four causes. He identified four explanations or causes: material, formal, efficient, and final, all of which Vermigli employs here so his reader can know what is meant by Divine Law. Laws are mandates (material explanation) of a spiritual nature (formal explanation) derived from the character of God (efficient explanation) that point us either to our failure or to Christ himself (final explanation).

sin, is universal and has bearing on everybody. Paul makes this point here and earlier declared it clearly, saying that knowledge of sin is through the Law [Rom. 3:20]. If you ask here why the Apostle did not instead say that through the Law is an awareness of righteousness, my answer is, because a person who is not yet regenerate is unable to have within himself an understanding of good works or of true righteousness that satisfies the Divine Law. And so, when such a one compares his deeds to the Law, he only finds failures and infractions.

Now, if we speak about the end of the Law that pertains to the elect, it is Christ. Paul makes this point as well when he says, "The end of the Law is Christ unto salvation" [Rom. 10:4]. He does not state this as a general point, however, but only for every believer. The Law itself *per se* does not even effect this end. The pagan philosophers taught that the end of the Law was the knowledge it produces of what actions ought to be done. As he is cited in the *Digest*, Chrysippus says the Law is the knowledge of things divine and human.[4] But this end and definition is too broad. All learning and all the liberal arts teach some knowledge of things divine and human.

It now remains to carefully consider what the material and efficient cause of the Law is. To be brief, I maintain that the Law is the mandate of God in which his will and character, or nature, are expressed. When I say *mandate*, I am speaking generically, as there are mandates of a people, a senate, kings, and emperors. But when I say *of God*, I am

---

4. *Digest* 1.3.2. Chrysippus, the founder of Stoicism, actually defines law (not *the* law) as "the king of all things," echoing a similar definition given by the poet Pindar (Frag. 151 [Böckh's edition]).

introducing a difference, one that indicates the efficient cause. As for my saying that God's will is revealed in the Law, this is a clear point that needs no explanation. However, my saying that in the Law we are informed about God's character and roused to the knowledge of his nature can perhaps seem rather perplexing. We will accordingly make it clear through examples.

In commanding us to love him, God is informing us that he has a nature deserving of love, since it is only right to love things that are worthy of being loved, and he would not enjoin upon us an ultimate good that we were to love, unless he himself were kindly disposed towards us. He therefore makes this exhortation because he desires us to be participants in himself. Thus we see that he has the qualities that he wants us to have. When he forbids us to kill, in the first place he is making known his will; in the second he is showing that he is a God who is averse to violence and the causing of harm and prefers rather to do good to men rather than afflict them with ills. By the same token these two ideas could be demonstrated in the other commandments as well. On the basis of this definition the points we made above about the formal and final cause of the Law can be deduced as well, inasmuch as a doctrine of this sort must necessarily be spiritual and produce no usual knowledge.

We are also taught that God has done men no trivial kindness through the Law, since it causes us to know ourselves and understand God's attributes. In the *Laws*, the *Republic*, and *Minos*, Plato comes to a definition of law as the correct system of governing, which directs everything to the best end through appropriate means by holding out penalties to those who break it and rewards to those who abide by it. This definition can be harmonized quite well with the Divine Law; indeed, such a law cannot but be from God. It is therefore no wonder that the ancient law-givers claimed some god as the author of their laws when they wanted them to be accepted. Minos claimed Jupiter as the author of his laws, Lycurgus Apollo, Solon and Draco Minerva, and Numa Pompilius Egeria. On the other hand, we know with certainty from Scripture that God gave our Law through Moses on Mount Sinai.

[CHAPTER 2: THE
MANICHEANS' ERROR]

2. Now that these points about the nature and definition of the Law have been established, we can easily see how disgraceful an error the Manicheans made when they scorned and reviled the Law as though it were evil. Since the Law only commands what ought to be commanded and forbids what ought to be forbidden, how can any just accusation be made against it? There cannot be found any just or honorable duty that is not endorsed in the Divine Law or any disgraceful and dishonorable one that is not banned in it. Moreover, since wicked acts are not only prohibited in the Law, but wicked desires as well, the Law shows that not only are our external acts to be corrected, but our mind and will are as well. A large part of our blessedness depends on coming to a knowledge of God, whereas philosophers so strongly recommend knowledge of ourselves. Hence, since God's Law provides both, as we have shown, it cannot be faulted as evil and detrimental without serious dishonor.

The passage where the Law is said to have entered so that sin might abound [Rom. 5:10] might seem to advocate for the Manicheans, just as the passage in Galatians, "the Law was established on account of transgressions" [Gal. 3:19], the passage in chapter seven of the present[1] letter, "Sin kills through the commandment" [Rom. 7:11], and the statement that is made in 2 Corinthians, "the Law is a function of death" [2 Cor. 3:7].

All these passages appear to corroborate the Manicheans' error, but it is important to carefully distinguish between what belongs to the Law essentially and what is associated with it incidentally. As we showed above, sin, death, condemnation, and other such things originate from the Law because of our sinful nature, but if you do not examine the Law against our character, but rather consider it in and of itself, or look at it against a sound and uncorrupted nature, you cannot make any conclusion about it but the one Paul makes, namely, that the Law is spiritual, holy, good, and established to give life. One should rather say that it points out sin rather than engenders it. If somebody by chance brought in a lamp to ugly people hiding in darkness, and they said to him, "Get out of here! Otherwise you will make us ugly with that light of yours!" we would hardly conclude from their words that light had the power and property to render people ugly. Rather, we would conclude that the things that are in and of themselves ugly are revealed and shown to be so by the light. This is precisely the case with the Law. It shines a light, so to speak, and brings to our awareness the sins that before were hiding.

But somebody will say, "If the Law is good and holy, why is it so displeasing and odious?" Because it calls peo-

---

1. I.e., Romans.

ple back from the things they are by nature predisposed to. They are grieved that those things are forbidden to them. When we look upon the Law, we see what we are supposed to do, and because of our inherent and innate pride, we would rather not be constrained by any rules. Next, we see that our actions are crookedly bent away from the uprightness that is held forth in the Law. What is more grievous, we find that we are too weak to be able to correct them and bring them back to the prescribed rule. Meanwhile, we look upon their penalty and God's wrath that we have incurred, and all of this so offends our spirit that we get angry, not at ourselves or our sins, as would be right, but at the Law God established, although it is otherwise utterly pure and holy.

However, this problem can be helped, and a change can be brought about so that things that until now were displeasing prove from now on pleasing. This will happen if we combine the Law with Christ. Just as the waters of Marah were thoroughly bitter to the people of Israel in the desert, yet when the piece of wood that God had specified was thrown in, these same waters became sweet [Exodus 15:25], so the Law, although bitter, when Christ is added, whom God set forth as our only Savior and the Law's due and rightful end, we will perceive that it is sweet. Psalm 119 marvelously sings the praises of God's Law and unmistakably shows how David had this experience: the Law is called delightful, pleasing, more delectable than honey and the comb.

Indeed, this is what is promised to us by the prophet, that God will write the Law on our hearts. This in effect means that he will give us the spirit of Christ so that through it we can be inclined to the things the Law has

commanded ought to be done, so that God's commandments can be delightful to our mind at least. The Apostle
also teaches this when he says, "In my mind I serve the
Law of God" [Rom. 7:25]. The regenerate experience this.
Although they are unable to render perfect obedience to
God's commandments, they nevertheless love and earnest-
ly desire them and cherish them as the highest good. They
constantly pray to God that they be able to come as near
as possible to accomplish them. As a result, it is apparent
how much the righteousness and usefulness of the Law
must be vindicated against the Manicheans.

[CHAPTER 3:
THE PELAGIANS' ERROR]

3. But conversely we must be on guard no less against the Pelagians who lay too much emphasis on the Law. They maintain that it is sufficient for salvation. They say that once people grasp what ought to be done they are able by sheer natural power to easily perform it. So as not to be condemned by the bishops of Palestine for completely rejecting the grace of God, Pelagius confessed it superficially. He affirmed that we need God's grace to be saved, but by *grace* he only meant our nature itself which God had given to us freely, inasmuch as we were made rational creatures by God endowed with free will. Additionally, he said that the Law, that is, instruction, was grace because on our own we do not know what we ought to do or believe unless God reveals it to us. For this reason, writing against Celestius in his *On the Grace of Christ* Augustine says that the Pelagians teach that the power of nature is helped by grace, but adds that if one examines and analyzes what they mean, they mean nothing else by grace, instruction, and Law than that man has sufficient power on his own

to fulfill God's commandments once he has but gained a knowledge of the Law.[1]

The Scholastics come very close to this error in their teaching that a person can keep God's commandments by his own sheer natural power as far as the substance of the work is concerned, yet not as far as the intention of the one who gives the commandment is concerned, by which they mean that we are able to perform the works themselves, just not as God commanded they be done—that is, out of love and the spirit. I suspect they added this second part so that it would look like they differed from the Pelagians in some way, but Augustine was so averse to such beliefs that he denies a perfect obedience to God's commandments even to the regenerate as long as they live in the body. This is clear in his *Retractions*.[2] And that Augustine was absolutely right Paul will make clear in chapter seven of the present letter.[3] If what Pelagius taught were the case, there would be no need for Christ's coming and his sacrificial death on the cross. These were given precisely because we were unable to attain to a righteousness of works by our own strength. Paul clearly asserts this when he says, "What was impossible for the Law because it was weakened through the flesh," etc. [Rom. 8:3].

This obviously shows that man was unable to fulfill the Law because of the weakness of his flesh. Paul adds,

---

1. Augustine, *De gratia Christi* 1.29 (*On the Grace of Christ, NPNF* 1/5:228).

2. E.g., Augustine, *Retractationes* 63.1, trans. Meredith Freeman Eller, in *The Retractationes of Saint Augustine*, Ph.D. diss. (Boston University, 1946), 298.

3. I.e., Romans.

"The wisdom of the flesh is enmity with God. For it is not subject to the Law of God, nor indeed can it be" [Rom. 8:7]. Even though the Law has the power to teach and enlighten the mind, it does not for all that supply the means or change the will. Accordingly, Ambrose says in his *Flight from the World*, "The Law can stop up the mouth of all, but cannot convert the mind," and, "The Law reveals sin, but does not remove wickedness."[4] Thus grace must be combined with the Law. Because the Pelagians put a low premium on grace they wandered away from their salvation and were rightly condemned by the Church.

4. Concerning the function of the Law these few points must be remembered: first, it is not entirely useless even before regeneration, since it can contribute to civil order. If people in one way or another do the external acts of the Law, even though to those who do them they are sins, civil society can still be maintained. Where there is no observance of these acts everything falls into confusion. Injustices are committed, wanton impulse runs riot, God's wrath is aroused to the point of not allowing governments thus corrupted to continue any longer. Yet there is another, more internal function of the Law. This pertains to the conscience. It accuses, impels, tortures, and condemns it without ceasing. This is the way God brings a person to justification, as we have pointed out. When this is obtained, not even then does the Law remain idle, but is like a mirror in which the regenerate can see what fruits of faith they ought to demonstrate, how far they are daily progressing, what they should give thanks for, and how far away they are from complete renewal, so that

---

4. Ambrose, *De fuga saeculi* 3.15 (*CSEL* 32:175).

they can more fervently beseech God for it. The Law also sets before their eyes a target that they should aim at in all their actions. Even though in this life they do not hit that target, they ought still to make every effort to miss it by a lesser margin. Thus it is seen how great an aid the Law is in our external actions, what it brings about in the conscience, and how great a help it is to the regenerate.

Guidelines Essential for Both Explicating and Obeying the Law

5. Only[5] an outline is set forth in the Ten Commandments, and a rather condensed and basic one at that, all the manifestations of which we are supposed to understand. The desire for more (πλεονεξία) is the main heading for acts of theft, just as in the case of more shameful acts of self-indulgence adultery is the only term used, but it includes all the categories of impurity. As far as idolatry is concerned, every kind of false worship is forbidden though only the one that is more blatant is expressed.

6. When[6] two commandments are set forth that are inconsistent with each other, the second is to be obeyed. God commanded that he be brought the first fruits and that sacrifices be made to his name [Exodus 22:29], but conversely he commanded later that all the property of

---

5. This section is taken from Vermigli's commentary on Romans 2, *In epistolam S. Pauli ad Romanos*, 61.

6. This section is taken from Vermigli's commentary on 1 Samuel (15:18), *In duos libros Samuelis commentarii* (Zürich: Froschauer, 1564), 87v.

the Amalekites should be utterly destroyed [1 Sam. 15:3]. Saul was supposed to obey this second commandment.

7. It[7] should be noted that in all commandments, be they ceremonial or judicial and moral, when two of God's commandments appear to be incompatible and the one to preclude the other so that both cannot be kept at the same time—indeed one of them must be disregarded for the moment—the one that is judged to be weightier and more compelling should be kept. However, the other one that is considered of lesser weight and moment is not broken because in this instance nothing is done contrary to the will of God. The Law commands that each person look after the welfare of his neighbor and, if somebody is in a position of authority, he should even put up armed defense of his community [Exodus 20:13]. Yet the Law also commands that no work is to be done on the Sabbath [Exodus 20:10]. An enemy lays siege to one's city, and on the Sabbath at that because he knows that this law was laid upon the citizens. There seems to be a conflict in the commandments here: on the one hand the community's welfare must be protected, on the other one has to keep the Sabbath. The Maccabees decided in favor of fighting because they held the safety of the state to be greater and more important than the Sabbath ritual [1 Mac. 2:38].

Similarly, there is a commandment that one who is hungry should be fed [Prov. 25:21], yet another commandment states that the showbread should not be eaten by any but the priests [Exodus 29:32]. David comes hungry to the priest, but he has nothing except the loaves of

---

7. This section is taken from Vermigli's commentary on Judges (11:11), *In librum Iudicum commentarii* (Zürich: Froschauer, 1561), 132v.

the Presence. Thus two conflicting commandments clash. The sensible priest obeys and carries out the more important commandment, namely, feeding the hungry. He brings out the loaves of the Presence and helps David [1 Sam. 21:6]. Likewise, there is a commandment to supply arms to the magistrate, since his subjects are supposed to help him.[8] Conversely, it was decreed that things consecrated to God are not to be employed for other purposes [Lev. 22:2]. David, the king's son-in-law and captain who waged wars on his behalf as commander of the army, did not at that time have any weapons. The priest had no arms at hand except the sword of Goliath. Here are two commandments that appear to be contrary. The priest follows the former one and gives his magistrate the sword because he believed it was better to arm his magistrate than observe a religious formality.[9]

Again, there is a commandment that the Church should not lack ministers to the point of being destitute of them. Another commandment in Paul says that a recent convert should not be made bishop. The church in Milan is in trouble and cannot find a suitable bishop who is both free of any Arianism and has great authority and learning bestowed upon him by God. There is one, Ambrose, but he is a recent convert and catechumen.[10] Here two commandments clash that are by all appearances contrary to each other, but it was right for the less important

---

8. No biblical citation is given for this claim by Vermigli.

9. Cf. 1 Sam. 21:9.

10. For the story of Ambrose's appointment, see Paulinus, *De vita Ambrosii* 6.

commandment to give ground to the more important. Speaking through the declaration of the prophet, Christ has taught us, "I desire mercy, not sacrifice" [Hosea 6:6]. He does not say he does not want sacrifice, but rather declares that if two commandments come into conflict, one of which pertains to mercy while the other to sacrifice, he prefers mercy over sacrifice.

8. The[11] question arises whether or not the old man in Judges 19:24 acted properly when he offered his daughter and the Levite's wife to the men of Gibeah so that they would not rape his guest [i.e., the Levite]. Everybody gives a different answer. Some say that he took into account the enormity and heinousness of the crime and opted for the lesser evil over the greater because he refused to betray the good faith he had extended his guest. Thus by this thought process they believe he can be excused. And they do not think any differently about Lot [Gen. 19:8]. In particular, Chrysostom heartily commends Lot in this episode, just as Ambrose does in his *De Abraham patriarcha*, on the grounds that he put the desecration of his own house second to so heinous a deed.[12]

However, examining the matter more carefully and closely in his *Questions on Genesis*, Augustine asserts that balancing sins against each other is wholly untenable.[13]

---

11. This section is taken from Vermigli's commentary on Judges (19:24 [London 1576 reads 19:14], *In librum Iudicum commentarii* [Zürich: Froschauer, 1561], 181v–182r).

12. Ambrose, *De Abraham patriarcha* 1.52 (*PL* 14:440).

13. Augustine, *Quaestiones in Genesim* 42 (= *Quaestiones in Heptateuchum* 42, PL 34:559). In fact, in the passage Vermigli cites at least, Augustine does not express a final opinion on the matter.

In his opinion, Lot did not have license to hand over his daughter to the Sodomites' lust so that they would not commit a more atrocious sin, nor are we allowed to commit a lesser misdeed to avoid a greater one. The reason is that the Apostle clearly teaches we are not to commit evils to achieve a good result [Rom. 3:8]. Therefore, when it comes to sin, total abstention is required, however insignificant it may seem, and if a more serious sin will seem to follow if we refuse that sin, we must commit the care of that issue to God; only we ought not to commit any sin on the basis of that pretext. This was Augustine's opinion, and I heartily accept it.

But not to depart from the story I brought up, although the old man owed good faith to his guest, he also owed good faith and protection to his daughter and the Levite's wife, nor was it permitted to him to show good faith to his guest beyond what the Word of God allowed. Consequently, he could not rightly prostitute his daughter or his guest's wife to those men. A father does not have such authority over his daughter that he can subject her to the lust of others, nor is the daughter under any obligation to obey her father in the case of sin if he so desires and gives such a command.

But one will say, "A lesser evil should be preferred over a greater one." I know this is commonly said, but it must be correctly understood as meant to be applicable in external afflictions and hardships of body and life. In troubles of this sort whenever we are forced to consider which of two things we prefer, we must prefer the lesser loss over the greater since an element of something good factors in. In the case of sin, however, no element of any good factors in, and of course whatever is sin must be rejected on the spot, come what may. Nevertheless, Augustine excuses Lot and the old man on the grounds that they erred because they were distressed and agitated. Prudent men often do things in an agitated state that they later disapprove of when once they regain their composure. But this excuse does not entirely exonerate these men of sin, though it does mitigate it somewhat.

If somebody says Paul chose the lesser sin over the greater when he said he preferred himself to be accursed and cut off (ἀνάθεμα) from Christ for the sake of his Jewish brothers than for them to continue in the blindness and stubbornness that held them down—whoever advances this argument against us should know that he fails to understand this passage in Paul correctly.[14] To be sure, the Apostle wanted to purchase the Jews' salvation at his own peril, at a loss and with a cost, but not with sin; namely, to be accursed and cut off (ἀνάθεμα) from Christ, not to the point of apostatizing or ceasing to believe in Christ, but of only not enjoying bliss and eternal life. Augustine writes a lot more against such balancing of sins one against another, and in particular:

> What if one demanded from an unwed girl that she consent to being defiled or from a married woman that she consent to adultery, and threatened to kill himself if he did not get what he wanted? Should good and chaste women consent to him? Of course not. Nor if he ends up killing himself ought the chaste women to be considered responsible for his death. They will

---

14. See Romans 9:3.

of course feel sorry for him, they will be sorrow-
ful over what has happened, but they will not
imagine they did anything wrong in not yielding
to his illicit demands.[15]

Similarly, on Psalm 146 Augustine writes, "If one refus-
es his wife her due intimacy so that he can live chastely,
and in the meantime the wife falls into adultery, he sins,
and his plan cannot be approved. He may not commit
sin vis-à-vis wife in order to practice chastity. God does
not requite such a wrong with that reward."[16] In this light
the pronouncement of Leo I, distinction forty-six, chapter *Non suo*, is commendable.[17] Here[18] he said, "It is not
becoming for people to employ their sin for other people's
gain." In his *De mendacio ad Consentium* Augustine says,
"One must do whatever he can for his neighbors' salvation, but if it comes to it that one cannot be helped except

---

15. This passage is not found in the works of Augustine. Vermigli,
though using direct speech, is evidently paraphrasing Augustine
broadly. Cf. *De civitate Dei* 1.16–21 (*City of God*, *NPNF* 1/2:12–15).

16. Again, Vermigli appears to be paraphrasing Augustine in direct
speech that does not occur verbatim in the latter's work, although the
germ of the idea might be detected there. Cf. Augustine, *Enarrationes
in psalmos* 146 (*Expositions on the Psalms*, *NPNF* 1/8:665).

17. The reference here is to the *Decretum Gratiani* (46.10: *Sicut suo*),
a twelfth-century compilation of canon law. It, along with five other
collections, formed the monumental *Corpus iuris canonici*, the basis
of canon law until 1917. See Anders Winoth, *The Making of Gratian's
Decretum* (Cambridge: Cambridge University Press, 2004), 1–33.

18. London 1576: *quae*. Judges 1561, Zürich 1580, and Heidelberg
1603: *qua*. The latter is the better reading.

through sinning, there is nothing left for us to do."[19] He adds, "Nobody is to be brought to Heaven through a lie." He also says elsewhere, "If poor people see a rich man who is cruel and greedy and decide to steal something from him to either help themselves or other poor folk they do not mitigate their sin, they increase it."[20] In his *Letter to Siagrius*, Gregory of Rome writes, "Committing a lesser sin to avoid a greater one is to give as a sacrifice to God a portion of one's misdeed, as it is written in Proverbs 21" [Prov. 21:27].[21] As for the fact that Chrysostom and Ambrose commend Lot on this account, they must be taken as approving of his care and fidelity to his guests and as taking into account the heinousness of the sin that the citizens were getting reading to commit, not that they approved of their prostituting their[22] women.

9. We[23] should note that all of God's requirements either command or forbid. They command not simply that

---

19. Regarding this and the following citation, while the sentiments can more or less be found in this work, the exact, or even near exact, phrasing cannot. Vermigli seems to be once again loosely paraphrasing his source with phraseology that appears to be a direct quote. Cf. Augustine, *De mendacio* 11 (*On Lying, NPNF* 1/3:463).

20. The translator has not been able to locate either these words or the sentiment in Augustine's works.

21. The translator has found no letter to Syagrius, Bishop of Autun, in which this sentiment is expressed. Vermigli's memory has possibly failed, or he was working from a collection (e.g., the *Decretum Gratiani*) which was erroneous at places.

22. "Their" (*eorum*) here suggests Vermigli has not just Lot in mind, but the old man of Judges 19 as well.

23. This section is taken from Vermigli's commentary on Romans 7,

something be casually done, but that it be done with all our soul, with all our heart, with all our strength, and with the utmost of care so that there will not be anything in us that is not in submission to God's will, whereas what they forbid they do not simply forbid that it not be found in us, but that not even a desire or propensity toward it be left remaining in us. This is the reason why God has decreed, "You shall not covet" [Exodus 20:17], so that we will be averse to those things God has forbidden in our mind, will—in short, in each and every part of our body and spirit. In this way these two commandments complement each other. The commandment, "You shall love the LORD your God with all your soul, with all your heart," etc. [Deut. 6:5], should be taken to apply to all requirements that command something, while the last one, "You shall not covet" [Exodus 6:17], is likewise to be understood in everything that is forbidden. For this reason, the actualization and, so to speak, soul of the Law are taken to reside in these two commandments on the grounds that without them all the other commandments of God cannot be fully realized.

In epistolam S. Pauli Apostoli ad Romanos, 229.

SELECT BIBLIOGRAPHY

Primary

Ambrose. *Hexameron, Paradise.* New York: Fathers of the Church, Inc., 1961.

Anselm. *The Major Works.* Edited by Brian Davies and G. R. Evans. Oxford: Oxford University Press, 1998.

Augustine. *Against Julian the Pelagian.* Translated by Matthew Schumacher. New York: Fathers of the Church, 1957.

————. *The Literal Meaning of Genesis.* Vol. 1, bks 1–6. Translated by John Hammond Taylor. New York: Paulist Press, 1982.

————. *Questions on the Heptateuch.* In *The Works of St. Augustine: A Translation for the 21st Century,* translated by Joseph T. Leinhard, SJ, and Sean Doyle. New York: Augustinian Heritage Institute, 2016.

————. *Saint Augustin: Anti-Pelagian Writings.* Translated by Peter Holmes, Robert Wallis, and Benjamin Warfield. 1ˢᵗ ser., vol. 5 of *Nicene and Post-Nicene Fathers,* edited by Philip Schaff. Grand Rapids, MI: Eerdmans, 1980 reprint.

————. *To Simplician, on various questions.* In *Augustine: Earlier Writings,* translated and edited by John H. S. Burleigh, 376–406. Philadelphia: The Westminster Press, 1953.

Basil of Caesarea, *St. Basil the Great: On the Human Condition*. Translated by Nonna Verna Harrison. Crestwood, NY: St. Vladimir's Seminary Press, 2005.

Calvin, John. *The Bondage and Liberation of the Will: A Defence of the Orthodox Doctrine of Human Choice against Pighius*. Edited by A. N. S. Lane. Translated by G. I. Davies. Grand Rapids, MI: Baker Books, 1996.

―――. *Institutes of the Christian Religion*. Translated by Ford Lewis Battles. Atlanta: John Knox Press, 1975.

Chrysostom. *Homilies on Genesis 1–17*. Translated by Robert C. Hill. Washington, D.C.: The Catholic University of America Press, 1986.

―――. *Homilies on Genesis 18–45*. Translated by Robert C. Hill. Washington, D.C.: The Catholic University of America Press, 1990.

Cyprian. *The Letters of Cyprian*. Vol. 3, Letters 55–66. Translated by G. W. Clarke. New York: Paulist Press, 1986.

Daneau, Lambert. *D. Aurelii Augustini Hiponensis Episcopi liber De haeresibus, ad Quodvultdeum . . . emendatus et commentariis illustratus, a quo eodem additae sunt haereses ab orbe condito ad constitutum Papismum et Mahumetismum, etiam ea quae hic erant ab Augustino praetermissae*. Geneva: Eustache Vignon, 1578.

Hugo of St. Victor. *On the Sacraments of the Christian Faith*. Translated by Roy Deferrari. College Station, PA: Penn State University Press, 1951.

Jerome. *Commentaries on the Twelve Prophets.* Translated by Thomas Scheck. Downers Grove, IL: InterVarsity Press, 2016.

Lombard, Peter. *The Sentences.* Translated by Guilio Silano. Toronto: Pontifical Institute of Medieval Studies, 2008.

Origen. *Commentary on the Epistle to the Romans.* Translated by Thomas Scheck. Washington, D.C.: The Catholic University of America Press, 2002.

Pighius, Albert. *De libero hominis arbitrio et divina gratia, Libri decem.* Cologne: Melchior Novesianus, 1542.

———. "De peccato originis controversia." In *Controversiarum praecipuarum in comitiis Ratisponensibus tractatarum et quibus nunc potissimum exagitatur Christi fides et religio, diligens, et luculenta explicatio.* Cologne: Melchior Novesianus, 1542, fols. iʳ–xxixʳ.

Vermigli, Peter Martyr. *In Epistolam S. Pauli Apostoli ad Romanos.* Zurich: [A. Gesner], 1559.

Secondary

Anderson, Marvin W. *Peter Martyr: A Reformer in Exile (1542–1562).* Nieuwkoop: B. de Graaf, 1975.

———. "Peter Martyr on Romans." *Scottish Journal of Theology* 26, no. 4 (1973): 401–20.

Backus, Irena and Aza Goudriaan. "*Semipelagianism*: The Origins of the Term and Its Passage into the History of Heresy." *Journal of Ecclesiastical History* 65, no. 1 (2014): 25–46.

Baschera, Luca. "Aristotle and Scholasticism." In *A Companion to Peter Martyr Vermigli*, edited by Torrance Kirby, Emidio Campi, and Frank James III, 133–60. Leiden: Brill, 2009.

———. "Peter Martyr Vermigli on Free Will: The Aristotelian Heritage of Reformed Theology." *Calvin Theological Journal* 42, no. 2 (2007): 325–46.

Beatrice, Pier Franco. *The Transmission of Sin: Augustine and the Pre-Augustinian Sources.* Translated by Adam Kamesar. Oxford: Oxford University Press, 2013.

Brady, Jules M. "St. Augustine's Theory of Seminal Reasons." *New Scholasticism* 38, no. 2 (1964): 141–58.

Campi, Emidio. "Genesis Commentary: Interpreting Creation." In *A Companion to Peter Martyr Vermigli*, edited by Torrance Kirby, Emidio Campi, and Frank James III, 209–30. Leiden: Brill, 2009.

Colish, Marcia. *Faith, Fiction, and Force in Medieval Baptismal Debates.* Washington, D.C.: The Catholic University of America Press, 2014.

Denlinger, Aaron. "Calvin's Understanding of Adam's Relationship to His Posterity: Recent Assertions of the Reformer's 'Federalism' Evaluated." *Calvin Theological Journal* 44, no. 2 (2009): 226–50.

Di Gangi, Mariano. *Peter Martyr Vermigli, 1499–1562: Renaissance Man, Reformation Master.* Lanham, MD: University Press of America, 1993.

Donnelly, John Patrick, SJ. *Calvinism and Scholasticism in Vermigli's Doctrine of Man and Grace.* Leiden: Brill, 1976.

————. "Peter Martyr on Fallen Man: A Protestant Scholastic View." PhD thesis, The University of Wisconsin-Madison, 1972.

Donnelly, John Patrick, SJ, Robert Kingdon, and Marvin Anderson. *A Bibliography of the Works of Peter Martyr Vermigli.* Ann Arbor, MI: Edwards Brothers, 1990.

Evans, Robert. *Pelagius: Inquiries and Reappraisals.* New York: The Seabury Press, 1968.

Faber, Jelle. "Imago Dei in Calvin: Calvin's Doctrine of Man as the Image of God in Connection with Sin and Restoration." In *Essays in Reformed Doctrine,* 227–50. Neerlandia, Alberta, Canada: Inheritance Publications, 1990.

Fedwick, Paul. *Basil of Caesarea: Christian, Humanist, Ascetic.* Toronto: Pontifical Institute of Mediaeval Studies, 1981.

Gousmett, Chris. "Creation Order and Miracle according to Augustine." *Evangelical Quarterly* 60, no. 3 (1988): 217–40.

Gross, Julius. *Geschichte des Erbsündendogmas: Ein Beitrag zur Geschichte des Problems vom Ursprung des Übels.* 4 vols. Munich: Ernst Reinhardt Verlag, 1960–72.

James, Frank III. "The Complex of Justification: Peter Martyr Vermigli versus Albert Pighius." In *Peter Martyr Vermigli: Humanism, Republicanism, Reformation,* edited by Emidio Campi, Frank James, and Peter Opitz, 45–58. Geneva: Droz, 2002.

Keech, Dominic. *The Anti-Pelagian Christology of Augustine of Hippo.* Oxford: Oxford University Press, 2012.

Landgraf, Artur Michael. "Die Vererbung der Sünden der Eltern auf die Kinder nach der Lehre des 12. Jahrhunderts." *Gregorianum* 21 (1940): 203–47.

Lane, Anthony. "Albert Pighius's Controversial Work on Original Sin." *Reformation and Renaissance Review* 4, no. 1 (2002): 29–61.

McLelland, Joseph C. "A Literary History of the *Loci communes*." In *A Companion to Peter Martyr Vermigli*, edited by Torrance Kirby, Emidio Campi, and Frank James III, 479–94. Leiden: Brill, 2009.

———. "Peter Martyr Vermigli: Scholastic or Humanist?" In *Peter Martyr Vermigli and Italian Reform*, edited by Joseph C. McLelland, 141–51. Waterloo, Ontario: Sir Wilfred Laurier University Press, 1980.

Pitkin, Barbara. "Nothing but Concupiscence: Calvin's Understanding of Sin and the *Via Augustini*." *Calvin Theological Journal* 34, no. 2 (1999): 347–69.

Rees, Brinley. *Pelagius: A Reluctant Heretic*. Wolfeboro, NH: The Boydell Press, 1988.

Steinmetz, David. "Peter Martyr Vermigli (1499–1562): The Eucharistic Sacrifice." In *Reformers in the Wings*, 151–61. Philadelphia: Fortress Press, 1971.

Strohm, Christoph. "Petrus Martyr Vermiglis *Loci communes* und Calvins *Institutio Christianae religionis*." In *A Companion to Peter Martyr Vermigli*, edited by Torrance Kirby, Emidio Campi, and Frank James III, 77–104. Leiden: Brill, 2009.

Vasoli, Cesare. "*Loci communes* and the Rhetorical and Dialectical Traditions." In *Peter Martyr Vermigli and*

Italian Reform, edited by Joseph C. McLelland, 17–28. Waterloo, Ontario: Sir Wilfred Laurier University Press, 1980.

Vorster, Nico. "Calvin's Modification of Augustine's Doctrine of Original Sin." In *Restoration through Redemption: John Calvin Revisited*, edited by Henk Belt, 45–61. Leiden: Brill, 2013.

Widengren, Geo. *Mani and Manichaeism*. New York: Holt, Rinehart, and Winston, 1965.

Williams, N. P. *The Ideas of the Fall and of Original Sin: A Historical and Critical Study*. London: Longmans, Green and Co., Ltd., 1927.

INDEX

A

Chrysippus, 120
Chrysostom, iv, 43–45, 110, 133, 137
Church, in Milan, 132
Cicero, ii, xvii–xviii, 8, 103–8, 115
circumcision, 32
  of hearts, 12
civil order, xx, 129
coercion, xvii, 17–20, 74, 105n7, 108–9, 111.
  See also violence, to will.
commandment(s), 15–16, 82, 83, 121, 124, 126, 128,
  131–33, 138
  ten, xxii, 130
conceived, as children of God, 39–41
concupiscence. *See* desire
conscience, 50, 70–71, 129–30
contingency, 107, 116
conversion, x, xiii, xiv, 51, 129, 132
Cornelius, xv, 30–33, 35–38, 40, 44–45, 57
Cotta, 104
curse, 12, 15, 67, 68, 69, 88
Cyclops, 102

D
David, 131–32
death, xvi, xx, 2, 5, 7, 15, 53, 84, 88, 90, 93, 95, 96,
  101–2, 103, 124, 128, 135
Decalogue, xxii, 130
deeds. *See* works
deliberation, v, vi, viii, 2, 8, 17, 76
depravity, 1, 11, 50, 54, 77, 81, 89, 90–91, 96

desire (concupiscence), ix–x, xiii, xvi, 2, 6, 7, 49, 51,
    76–77, 81–85, 87, 89, 90, 91, 96, 98, 123, 130,
    138
divination, 103, 106
Donatists, 32
Donnelly, John Patrick, xixn26, xxiiin29
Draco, 122
Duns Scotus, viii

E
Egeria, 122
Egypt, 49
elect, viii, 36, 53–54, 120
emotion, 76, 89–90, 112
empire(s), 47, 50
enemies, 24, 27, 39, 103, 131
Engammare, Max, 9n3
Epimenedes, 69n9
eternal life/death, 24, 47, 53, 59, 69, 88, 96, 135
Euripides, 116
evil, xvi, xvii, xx, 10, 21, 26, 27–28, 58, 66, 77, 87,
    93–94, 105n7, 110, 123. *See also* sin.
    lesser, 133–37

F
faith, xiii, xv, xvi, 20, 25–26, 29, 32–34, 35–38, 40, 41,
    43–45, 48, 57, 61, 62–66, 69–72, 77, 102, 129
Fall, in1, 10, 65
fate, 100, 101, 107, 116
first man. *See* Adam.
flesh, 10, 11–12, 61–62, 77, 83, 84, 93, 97, 128–29

publican, 57
punishment, xvi, 50, 90–91,

Q
Quintillian, ii
Quintus, 103

R
Radical Reformation, xxi
rebirth, x, xv, 3, 19, 25, 26, 30, 31, 57, 68, 69, 84, 95,
    96
regeneration, xii, xiii, 36, 39, 40, 53, 62, 65, 74, 75–79,
    81, 83, 88, 95, 96, 119, 120, 126, 128, 129, 130
remuneration, 47, 49
repentance, 51, 58
reprobate, 54
Reuter, Mark, 24n3
reward, 47–50, 121, 136
righteousness, 25, 26–27, 45, 59, 84, 120, 126, 128
    of God, 51, 54
Romans, 47–48

S
Saarinen, Risto, xiiin18
Sabbath, 131
sacraments,   38, 40, 41. *See also* baptism
sacrifice, 73, 75, 128, 130, 133, 137
saints, x, 18, 44, 58, 83

venial, 87, 88n2
slave/slavery
  to righteousness, 27
  to sin, i, 9, 11, 19, 26–27, 74, 77
Socrates, v, xi, 24
Solon, 7, 122
Sophists, 57
soul(s), xvi, 23n2, 41, 44, 51, 109, 138
Souter, Alexander, 72n12
spirits, blessed, 18
spontaneous, definition of, 20
Stoics, Stoicism, 50, 61n1, 107, 116, 120n4
Syagrius/Siagrius, Bishop of Autum, 137

T
Tertullian, 84
thief on the cross, 41, 44
Thomas à Kempis, xxi
Thomas Aquinas, viii, 90n3
Timothy, 78
trees, good or bad, 25, 63–68, 74, 75–76

U
unbelievers, xvi, 64, 70, 73
ungodly, 11, 20, 25, 32, 51, 75, 78, 98
unregenerate, 19, 24, 51, 54, 98
unrepentant, 68, 90

V
Valla, Lorenzo, iii, xixn25

MORE FROM DAVENANT PRESS

INTRODUCTION TO PROTESTANT THEOLOGY

- *Reformation Theology: A Reader of Primary Sources with Introductions*
- *Grace Worth Fighting For: Recapturing the Vision of God's Grace in the Canons of Dordt*

PETER MARTYR VERMIGLI LIBRARY

- *Dialogue on the Two Natures in Christ*
- *Philosophical Works: On the Relation of Philosophy to Theology*
- *The Oxford Treatise and Disputation on the Eucharist, 1549*
- *Predestination and Justification: Two Theological Loci*

VERMIGLI'S COMMON PLACES

- *On Original Sin (Vol. 1)*
- *On Free Will and the Law (Vol. 2)*

LIBRARY OF EARLY ENGLISH PROTESTANTISM

- *James Ussher and a Reformed Episcopal Church: Sermons and Treatises on Ecclesiology*
- *The Apology of the Church of England*
- *Jurisdiction Regal, Episcopal, Papal*
- *Radicalism: When Reform Becomes Revolution*
- *Divine Law and Human Nature*

- *The Word of God and the Words of Man*
- *In Defense of Reformed Catholic Worship*
- *A Learned Discourse on Justification*
- *The Laws of Ecclesiastical Polity: In Modern English, Vol. 1 (Preface–Book IV)*
- *The Shining Human Creature: Christian Ethics Vol. 1*
- *Made like the Maker: Christian Ethics Vol. 2*
- *A Treatise on Christian Moderation*
- *The Word Made Flesh: A Treatise on Christology and the Sacraments from Hooker's Laws*

DAVENANT GUIDES

- *Jesus and Pacifism: An Exegetical and Historical Investigation*
- *The Two Kingdoms: A Guide for the Perplexed*
- *Natural Law: A Brief Introduction and Biblical Defense*
- *Natural Theology: A Biblical and Historical Introduction and Defense*

AMERICAN THEOLOGY SERIES

- *Communicating God's Trinitarian Fullness: A Commentary on Jonathan Edwards' End for Which God Created the World*
- *Religion and Republic: Christian American from the Founding to the Civil War*

DAVENANT RETRIEVALS

- *A Protestant Christendom?*
  The World the Reformation Made
- *People of the Promise:*
  A Mere Protestant Ecclesiology
- *Philosophy and the Christian:*
  The Quest for Wisdom in the Light of Christ
- *The Lord Is One: Reclaiming Divine Simplicity*

CONVIVIUM PROCEEDINGS

- *For the Healing of the Nations: Essays on Creation,*
  Redemption, and Neo-Calvinism
- *For Law and for Liberty: Essays on the Legacy of*
  Protestant Political Thought
- *Beyond Calvin: Essays on the Diversity*
  of the Reformed Tradition
- *God of Our Fathers: Classical Theism*
  for the Contemporary Church
- *Reforming the Catholic Tradition:*
  The Whole Word for the Whole Church
- *Reforming Classical Education:*
  Toward A New Paradigm

OTHER PUBLICATIONS

- *Enduring Divine Absence:*
  The Challenge of Modern Atheism
- *Without Excuse: Scripture, Reason,*
  and Presuppositional Apologetics

- *Being A Pastor: Pastoral Treatises of John Wycliffe*
- *Serious Comedy: The Philosophical and Theological Significance of Tragic and Comic Writing in the Western Tradition*
- *Protestant Social Teaching: An Introduction*
- *Begotten or Made?*
- *Why Do Protestants Convert?*

ABOUT THE DAVENANT INSTITUTE

The Davenant Institute aims to retrieve the riches of classical Protestantism in order to renew and build up the contemporary church: building networks of friendship and collaboration among evangelical scholars committed to Protestant resourcement, publishing resources old and new, and offering training and discipleship for Christians thirsting after wisdom.

We are a nonprofit organization supported by your tax-deductible gifts. Learn more about us, and donate, at www.davenantinstitute.org.

Made in the USA
Monee, IL
15 September 2024

65830852R00115